FLORAL KNITS

FLORAL KNITS

NOLA THEISS & CHRIS RANKIN

A Sterling/Lark Book
Sterling Publishing Co., Inc.   New York

Editor: Dawn Cusick
Design: Marcia Winters
Production: Marcia Winters, Sandra Montgomery
  and Elaine Thompson
Illustrations: Sandra Montgomery
Technical assistance: Diane Murphy, Jennifer Barr, Terry Zalenski

Library of Congress Cataloging-in-Publication Data: Available

10   9   8   7   6   5   4   3   2   1

A Sterling/Lark Book

Produced by Altamont Press, Inc.
  50 College Street, Asheville, NC 28801

First paperback edition published in 1992 by
  Sterling Publishing Company, Inc.
  387 Park Avenue South, New York, N.Y. 10016

English translation by Networks, Inc.
© 1991 by Altamont Press
  Photos and instructions © Ariadne/Eska Tijdscriften
  Utrecht, Holland
Text © 1991 by David Schoonmaker & Bruce Woods

Distributed in Canada by Sterling Publishing
% Canadian Manda Group, P.O. Box 920, Station U
  Toronto, Ontario, Canada M8Z 5P9
Distributed in Great Britain and Europe by Cassell PLC
  Villiers House, 41/47 Strand, London WC2N 5JE, England
Distributed in Australia by Capricorn Link Ltd.
  P.O. Box 665, Lane Cove, NSW 2066

Sterling   ISBN 0-8069-8366-3   Trade
                    0-8069-8367-1   Paper

CONTENTS

INTRODUCTION

Always in search of beautiful motifs to make their sweaters unique and special, sweater designers often take their inspiration from the world around them. One of the most popular and obvious inspirations is the flower, probably because of its variety, abundance, color range and intrinsic beauty. Even if designers were limited to one type of flower, such as the rose, they could knit and embroider an almost infinite number of designs. In this book, which includes flower motifs ranging from whimsical wildflowers to fantastic formal bouquets, almost half of the designs include roses and none of them are alike!

The idea of floral sweaters is sweetly old-fashioned and very romantic and many of these sweaters have a very feminine, delicate look. Some of the sweaters, though, are decidedly modern in their use of bright colors, abstract renditions, and their juxtaposition of flowers and geometry.

The language of flowers is universal, and its many messages are understood around the world. Many of these floral designs have a European flair to them. They have been collected from the best of Europe's designers. Their inspiration comes not only from the countryside and parlors of Europe, but also the tropics, the Far East, and even South America. And gardeners will have fun identifying various types of familiar flowers as well as seeing new types of flowers.

Many of these sweaters can be worn through the year and have been photographed in outdoor settings to enhance their floral feeling. Some of the sweaters are appropriate for a garden party, while others are perfect for the ski slope. Summer sweaters to be worn on the beach or as swimsuit coverups are often knit in cotton because of its cool feel against the skin and its easy washability.

The variety of shapes and designs in this book will give you a complete wardrobe of sweater styles. Beautiful oversized jackets are perfect for in-between season activities: a Fall bike ride or a Spring picnic. Classically shaped cardigans and vests complement the clothes beneath them. Oversized pullovers are perfect for the winter while cap-sleeve and short sleeve tops will be cool additions to your summer wardrobe.

Knitting lends itself beautifully to reproducing flower motifs. A variety of techniques can be used depending on the placement, the size, and the detail required. While these instructions are written for the hand knitter, the machine knitter will find it simple to adapt the simple shapes to the machine, using the assembly diagrams as a guide. In all cases, a chart is used to position the flower motifs. Large motifs can be knit in using the intarsia technique. Small repeated motifs can be knit in the fairisle style. Details or even whole motifs can be embroidered later in duplicate stitch or by using a selection of embroidery stitches. Embroidery can also be worked on store-bought sweaters so that even the non-knitter can make a floral sweater. Each of these techniques will be described in detail in the how-to section which follows.

This book is filled with gorgeous designs, but you should not feel obliged to reproduce them exactly. If you prefer the shape of one sweater, but the flower on another, simply adapt the motif. The only rule to borrowing a motif from one sweater to use for another is that their gauges should be very close so that the flower's proportions will remain the same. Feel free to change colors, simplify the design, or add detail. A friend of mine once made a beautiful full-length mohair coat with gorgeous pond flowers and foliage. She added little silver dragonflies which were not in the original design, and they brightened up the whole coat. You too can add your own personal touches and make your wardrobe a bouquet of floral sweaters.

BASIC INSTRUCTIONS

KNITTING WITH TWO OR MORE COLORS

Most knitters are surprised to discover that knitting with two or more colors is easier than it looks. It can be done with a single technique or by combining several different techniques. European knitters refer to any color change technique as "jacquard knitting," in honor of J. M. Jacquard, the French inventor who developed a knitting machine that used punch cards to change colors. Included under the generic heading of jacquard knitting is intarsia knitting, jacquard knitting, and many combinations of the two. The basic difference between these techniques hinges on whether the unused yarn is carried across the wrong side of the stitches in another color (intarsia), or whether two colors are crossed at their juncture (fairisle). This distinction is especially apparent to machine knitters because intarsia knitting requires a different carriage, while fairisle knitting uses the standard carriage and punch cards or electronic charting.

Most color knitting and embroidery is done on a flat stitch surface, usually the stockinette stitch. The stockinette stitch is knit on the right side and purled on the wrong side. Most of these patterns are worked exclusively in the stockinette stitch, though some patterns also use the reverse stockinette stitch to form ridges, relief stripes, or patterns. The reverse stockinette stitch is purled on the right side and knit on the wrong side. Most sweaters are designed using a 1/1 or 2/2 ribbing for the borders. To work a ribbing, alternately knit and purl every stitch (1/1) or every two stitches (2/2) and knit each following row as established. If another stitch is used in a pattern, complete instructions are given.

Color can also be added to fin-

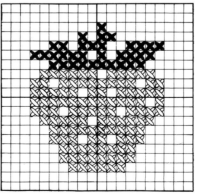

Cross stitch embroidery

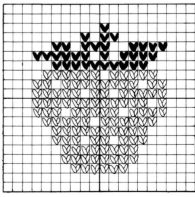

Duplicate stitch embroidery

ished knitting by using embroidery or crochet stripes on knit fabric. The most common kind of embroidery is duplicate stitch, also called Swiss darning, although any kind of embroidery, including cross stitch, can be worked on knit fabric as long as some simple techniques to avoid stretching are employed. A crochet hook can make simple vertical stripes, which is a lot easier than knitting in vertical stripes with single stitches.

CHARTS AND GAUGE

Just about all color change patterns, whether they are knitted in, embroidered, or crocheted on top of fin-

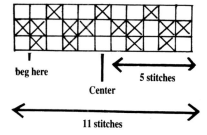

To center an 11 st chart over 35 stitches

beg here

Center   5 stitches

11 stitches

ished work require the use of a chart. Charts are read from the lower right corner to the left, unless otherwise specified. In some cases, an arrow will be used to indicate where to begin or where to center a chart. To determine where to start a row when you only know the center stitch, mark the center stitch of your knitting and count back to the beginning of the row. Count from the center of the chart on row 1 to

the beginning of row. When you have the same number of stitches on the chart as on your knitting, begin there. If you don't have enough stitches on the chart to cover your actual stitches, resume counting from the left end of row 1 toward the right end. For example, if your chart has 11 stitches and the 6th stitch is marked as the center and you have 35 stitches on your needle, you will have 17 stitches at each side of the center stitch. You have 5 stitches at the right of the center stitch; begin counting again from the left end of the chart. After one full repeat, return to the left edge of the chart and count back one stitch. This equals 17 stitches. Begin your knitting at this point. Often the beginning stitch for the different sizes will be indicated on the chart. You may be asked to repeat between one point and another on a chart a certain number of times and then between two other points to finish the row. If you read carefully, this is easy to do. A special note to machine knitters: Since your knitting will always have the wrong side facing you on the machine, remember to begin charts on the opposite side indicated in the hand knitting instructions.

You may or may not be required to work a border stitch at each edge of the chart. A border stitch is usually knit in Stockinette stitch to make it easy to sew into a seam. It is usually knit in the background color or in the same color as the adjacent stitch. Since it will only be part of the seam allowance, its color doesn't matter. The main

function of border stitches is to prevent any part of the motif to disappear into a seam.

Since a chart represents a certain amount of stitches and rows, it is crucial that you get the stitch and row gauge given in the pattern or the chart will not fit and the proportion of the motif may significantly change. In some kinds of knitting, row gauge may not be very significant, since we usually consider size a function of width. In these cases, length can easily be adjusted by adding or subtracting rows, but in any kind of color change pattern, the difference of a few rows is highly significant.

If your gauge is 20 stitches x 30 rows in 4", each stitch is one third wider than it is long. If you want to form a square, you have to knit a multiple of 2 stitches and 3 rows. If you have a gauge of 20 stitches x 25 rows in 4" and want to form a square, you would have to use a multiple of 2 sts and 2.5 rows. If you followed a chart for the first gauge on a piece knitted to the second gauge, your designs would be elongated. Keep this in mind if you cannot get the gauge called for in the pattern and make adjustments as you go. (This is much easier in embroidery since you can easily pull out a few stitches if they don't look right as opposed to pulling out a few dozen rows if you notice that something looks funny after you have completed knitting a large motif.)

FAIRISLE KNITTING

True fairisle knitting is always done in the round, but the term is commonly used to refer to any stranded color change technique. A stranded technique requires the use of more than one color in a row. Stitches in one color are knit, then a new color is introduced. The yarn color not being used is loosely carried across the wrong side of the work. A chart is used to determine which color is used for which stitches.

The hardest part of fairisle knitting is maintaining the proper tension when changing colors. The easiest way to do that is to continually spread out the stitches of the color just knit so that you have allowed enough yarn to stretch across the wrong side of the work without pulling. After you have completed one color, drop it, pick up the next color, and continue knitting. Take care not to cross the new color of yarn with the yarn just knit; instead just lay it next to the previous color. For example, if you were knitting in red and blue, you would try to always lay the red yarn over the blue or vice versa. If you do cross the yarns, they will become very tangled. One of the advantages of machine knitting intarsia designs is that the carriage maintains an even tension on the strands on the wrong side of the work. However, these strands may be very long and, unlike hand knitting, will not be woven in. Take care to select a pattern with no more than four or five stitches between colors.

One of the "rules" of fairisle knitting is to never use more than two colors in a row. This rule can be violated, but it is hard to maintain the

correct tension, and the knitting becomes extremely bulky when too many strands are carried across the wrong side of the work. If you are working with a fine yarn, however, bulk may not be a drawback. Remember also that if you want to use more than two colors in a row, you can use duplicate stitch embroidery to add a color over a stitch. Since you can introduce two new colors in every row, the number of colors used in a sweater is practically limitless.

Another "rule" is to never knit more than four or five neighboring stitches in one color because it is too difficult to maintain the proper tension on the carried yarn. Tension can

be maintained by weaving in the carried yarn. Simply hold it flat against the back of the work and use the running strand you are knitting with to catch the unused color. Check the work periodically because a highly contrasting color may show through the front of the work. You must be very careful about your tension so the stitches don't appear pulled. At the end of the row, the yarn should be carried along the seam edges, allowing enough give in the yarn so it doesn't pull up the rows.

In most cases the fairisle technique is worked in the stockinette stitch (knit right side of work rows, purl wrong side of work rows)

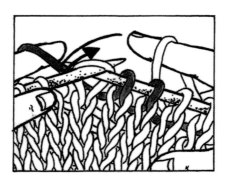
Knitting with right hand, stranding with left

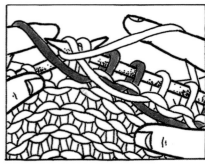
Purling with right hand, stranding with left

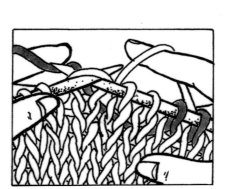
Knitting with left hand, stranding with right

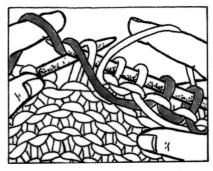
Purling with left hand, stranding with right

because the smooth background is an ideal backdrop for color. When you alternately knit and purl stitches, the yarn change from the previous row will show—half of the stitch will be in one color and half in the second color. To avoid this, always work the first row of the new color in the stockinette stitch. Many of these patterns use a striped ribbing. To create a smooth transition from one color to another, knit the first row of a new color on the right side of the work. The ribbing of the previous and following rows will make this row look like ribbing.

Sometimes you may want to use a color for only one row. The result of this is that the ball of the completed color will hang at the opposite end of the row from where you began. If you work back and forth on a double pointed circular needle, you can begin knitting at either end, wherever the color you want is hanging. This prevents a lot of cutting and tying on of colors and amazingly doesn't alter the appearance of the finished work. Just be sure to always knit the right side of work rows and purl the wrong side for the stockinette stitch.

INTARSIA KNITTING

Intarsia knitting is like painting with yarn. Each section of color is considered separate from the surrounding color. Usually the different colored sections of the designs are larger than a few stitches and may continue vertically or diagonally across the knitting, while a fairisle design is primarily horizontal. The back side of intarsia knitting is neat and unstranded and the bulk is much less than a similar fairisle design. Machine knitting intarsia requires the use of an intarsia carriage and much hand work of laying yarn across the needles, but it is still faster than hand knitting.

The main difficulty with intarsia knitting is keeping the different color yarns from becoming tangled. Often bobbins are used because they

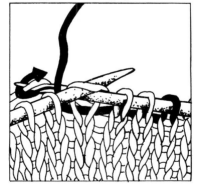

Crossing yarns when changing colors on knit rows

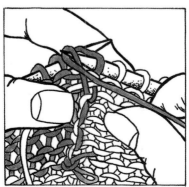

Crossing yarns when changing colors on purl rows

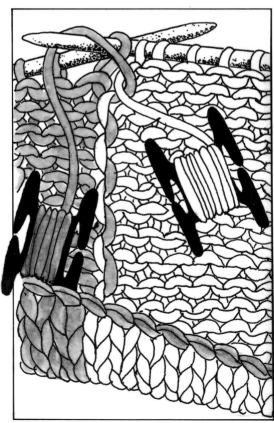

Using bobbins for intarsia knitting

allow only short lengths of yarn to be free. If you are working with many colors at a time, you can leave long strands of each color hanging loose, unballed or bobbined. Since there is no obstruction at the end, the strands can be untangled relatively easily. Don't try this with mohair or other yarns which like to cuddle up with each other or you will spend more time untangling than knitting. Some inventions developed to deal with this problem include boxes with separate compartments for each ball of yarn. You can also put each ball of yarn in a plastic bag with a wire tie to keep it closed. Then the yarn can only tangle with the length that's not in the bag. To keep the yarn from tangling at the end of rows, be systematic: turn to the left at the end of purl rows, turn to the right for knit rows.

Often intarsia knitting becomes fairisle knitting when the same color is used for two motifs near each other. Rather than using a separate ball for each section, you may want to carry the strand across the connecting stitches. In that case, you must use care to maintain the proper tension on the unused yarn just as in fairisle knitting.

EMBROIDERY
Some people have a real fear of knitting with color, perhaps because they've seen too many tangled messes of yarn or puckered up sur-

Duplicate stitch pocket motif

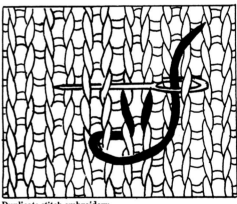

Duplicate stitch embroidery

ABBREVIATIONS

inc = increase
dec = decrease
St st = Stockinette stitch
beg = begin(ning)
foll = follow(ing)
pat = pattern
sts = stitches
MC = main color
CC = contrasting color
tog = together

faces on sweaters. Following the techniques above, neither of these disasters has to happen, but you may prefer to add color using embroidery. It can be used to embellish a knit-in motif or design, or it may be the entire method of "colorizing" a sweater. Often a pattern stitch will be knit in and then embroidery added to the finished work. Other times, embroidery will add a third or fourth color to a row of two colored fairisle knitting to avoid the bulk of carrying extra colors. Sometimes stripes or a simple fairisle motif will be knit in to create a background, and embroidered flowers will splash across the repeated stripes or motifs.

DUPLICATE STITCH EMBROIDERY
Duplicate stitch embroidery duplicates the stitch of the knitting by covering up the original stitch. It can be worked with the same kind of yarn as the original knitting, or with cotton embroidery floss or tapestry wool. In many cases, especially when using highly contrasting colors or yarns of different weight, parts of the original stitch will show through, but this can make the outline of the motif more soft and shaded looking, especially appropriate for floral motifs.

Duplicate stitch embroidery is done with a blunt tip, large-eyed needle, usually called a yarn or tapestry needle. Insert the threaded needle from the wrong side to the right side at the base of the stitch. Next, insert the needle under the two strands of the base of the stitch above and pull through, then insert

needle at the same point as the entry. Adjust the tension on the thread so as to cover the stitch below.

If you are working many stitches in a row, it is best to work across the row, then move one stitch up and work in the opposite direction across the row above. In some cases, you will work vertically rather than horizontally. There really is no problem working in any direction you like as long as you frequently check the back of the work to make sure your chosen method is neat. This is especially important on a cardigan where other people can see the inside of the sweater. Carrying strands of yarn over many stitches to get to the next section will give the back a messy appearance.

OTHER EMBROIDERY STITCHES
There are hundreds of embroidery stitches that can be worked on a knit fabric. They can be worked free-hand, without reference to the original knit stitches, or you can use tissue paper, tearaway fabric, or woven fabric such as Aida cloth or linen. In some cases, the instructions call for the design to be sketched on the paper and then pinned to the fabric. Basting thread is used to outline the design, and the paper is removed. In other cases, woven cloth is pinned to the knit fabric and embroidery is worked through both thicknesses, then the woven material which is unembroidered is cut away.

Always use the written instructions and the chart as a guide. There is no reason to exactly repro-

duce the original design. You may want to change the colors, the placement of the motif, or the stitches used. Following is a description of the stitches used in this book, but you may want to use other stitches. Feel free!

CROSS STITCH: Working from back to front, insert the needle between two stitches under the strand connecting the two stitches; cross the stitch diagonally to the right and insert needle behind the strand between stitches. Cross the

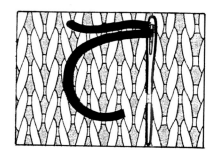

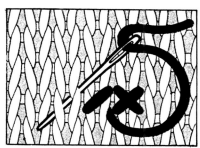

Cross Stitch

same stitch diagonally to the left and insert needle behind the strand between stitches. To work the next stitch, continue in the same way.

CHAIN STITCH: This stitch is used to make lines such as stems or to make petals on daisies and other flowers. Working from back to front, come up at a point and reinsert the needle at the same point, making a loop. With your finger, hold the top of the loop against the work at the desired point. Reinsert the needle inside the loop and make a small stitch to hold the top of the

loop. To make a line, reinsert the needle at the top of the loop and begin the next chain. To make flower petals, work single loops as indicated on a chart.

STEM STITCH: The stem stitch is used, surprisingly, to make stems or other lines which can easily turn direction or form curves. Working from back to front, come up at one point, go to wrong side a short distance later. Bring the needle to the front halfway on the first stitch. Insert the needle the same distance as the previous stitch and continue as before.

OUTLINE STITCH: The outline stitch is used to surround embroidered areas or to make lines as part of a motif. It is also called a back stitch when one stitch follows another. It is the easiest stitch to make. Working from back to front, come up at one point, and go down to the wrong side a short distance later.

SATIN STITCH: The satin stitch is used to fill in an area of a motif. It is easiest to work from the widest section and work to the narrowest section. The satin stitch is a combination

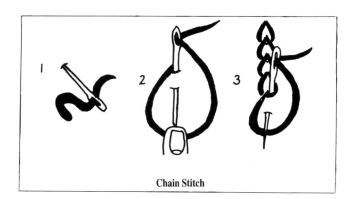

Chain Stitch

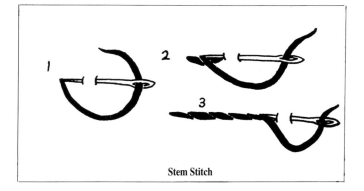

Stem Stitch

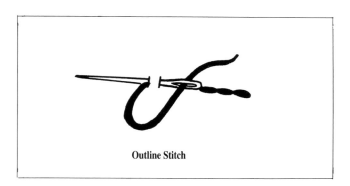

Outline Stitch

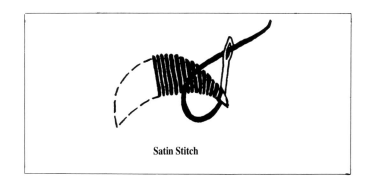

Satin Stitch

of many outline stitches. Working from back to front, come up at one point, go down to the wrong side at the designated point. As close as possible to the original insertion point, come up again and repeat until the entire area is filled in.

FRENCH KNOT: French knots are used as the centers of flowers, as buds, or wherever a raised spot of color is required. Working from back to front, come up at one point, twist yarn around needle once and reinsert needle at the same point.

BULLION STITCH: The bullion stitch is like a long French knot. Working from back to front, insert needle at beginning of line to be covered and reinsert at the end of the line, leaving a loop. Reinsert the needle at the beginning point and twist around the loop of yarn, pull the needle through the twists and insert the needle at the point where the twisted yarn will lie flat against the fabric.

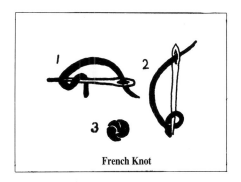
French Knot

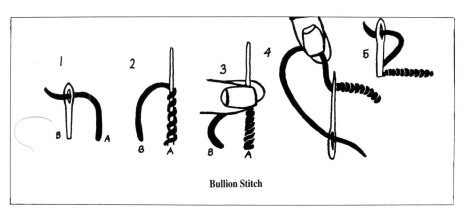
Bullion Stitch

CROCHETED STRIPES

Crocheted chain stitch stripes are worked on knit fabrics because they are so much easier to add to finished knitting than to knit in as single stitches. When worked over a flat surface, they also give a raised effect on the surface, or can blend in when reverse stockinette vertical stripes are knit into a design. The crocheted stripes then are worked over the purl stitches, bringing them up to the level of the knitted stitches.

Hold the yarn on the wrong side of the work and insert the crochet hook to wrong side of work. Pull up a loop of yarn. Reinsert the hook 1 row above the original point and pull up another loop. Draw the 2nd loop through the first and continue in this way. Unless a pattern indicates otherwise, each crocheted loop should be 1 row long.

Crocheting may also be used to make simple edgings on necks or front edges in single crochet or shrimp stitch.

Single crochet (sc): Insert hook into the 2nd chain from the hook. Wrap the yarn around the hook from back to front. Draw the yarn through the chain making 2 loops on the hook. Wrap yarn around hook and pull through 2 loops on hook. One single crochet stitch has been completed. Continue by inserting the hook in the next chain. After the last stitch, chain 2 and turn; insert the hook into the first stitch to begin the next row.

Shrimp stitch: Worked like single crochet, but worked in the opposite direction, that is, left to right, instead of right to left. Keep the right side of the work facing you as you work.

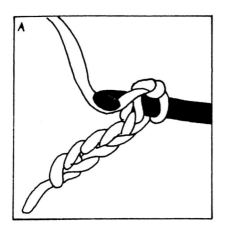
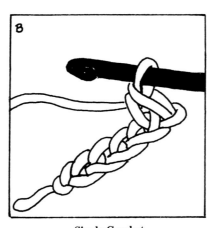
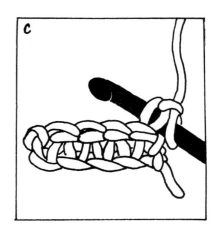

Single Crochet

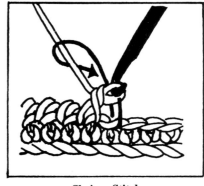

Shrimp Stitch

CONVERSION CHART OF KNITTING NEEDLE SIZES

■ The needle sizes given in the patterns are recommended starting points for making tension samples. The needle size actually used should be that on which the stated tension is obtained.

United States (US)	0	1	2	3	4	5	6	7	8	9	10	10.5	11	13	15
United Kingdom (UK)	14	13	12	11	10	9	8	7	6	5	4	2	1	00	0000
Metric (MM)			2	2.25	2.75	3	3.25	3.75	4	4.5	5	5.5	6	7	7.5	9	11

The level of difficulty for each project is indicated in the top left corner of the box that introduces each sweater.

One daisy (✿) equals simple stitches, simple shapes, and/or simple embroidery.

Two daisies (✿✿) equal moderately difficult pattern stitches, colorwork, and/or embroidery.

Three daisies (✿✿✿) equal complicated pattern stitches, intricate colorwork, and/or fancy embroidery.

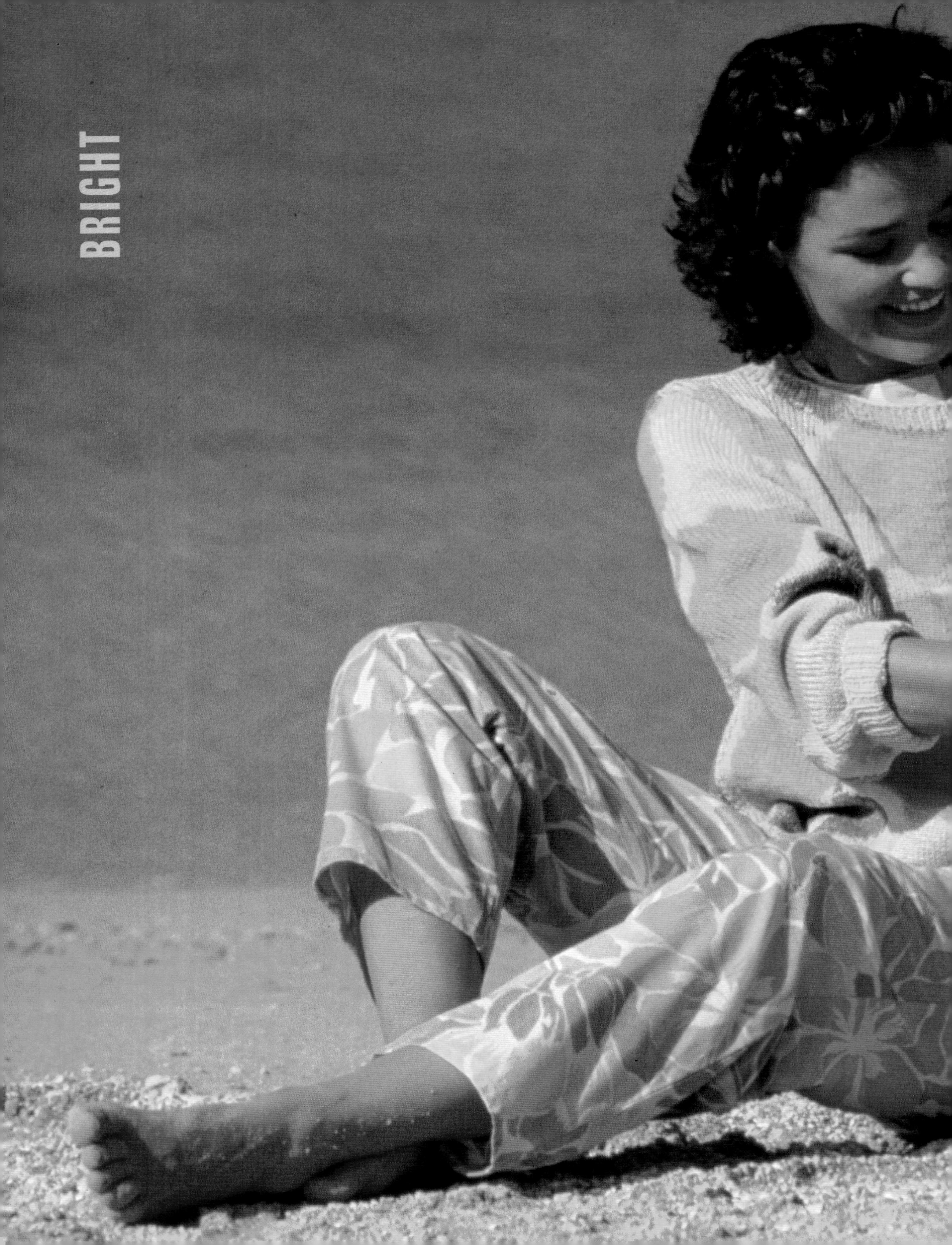
BRIGHT

Summer

BRIGHT

Summer sweaters with large flower motifs are the perfect choice for a day at the beach.

WOMAN'S PULLOVER

SIZES
- Small (Medium, Large)
- Finished bust measurements: 41" (44", 47")
- Finished length: 24-1/2"
- Finished sleeve length: 17-3/4"

MATERIALS
- Neveda Valentine (50 g): 12 (13, 14) balls Light Rose - MC; Embroidery: 4 balls Dark Rose - A; 3 balls Green - B; 2 balls each Salmon - C and Blue - D; 1 ball Yellow - E
- U.S. size 4 and 6 knitting needles. Circular needle U.S. size 4. (Metric sizes: 3.5, 4.0, and 3.5 circular.)

GAUGE
U.S. size 6 needles in St st: 4" (10 cm.) = 20 sts x 26 rows.
To save time, take time to check gauge!

BACK
With smaller size needles and MC, cast on 90 (96, 102) sts and work 2-1/2" in 1/1 ribbing. Purl 1 row across wrong side of work, inc 16 (18, 20) sts evenly spaced across row = 106 (114, 122) sts.
Change to larger size needles, work in St st.
Shape Armholes: When back measures 14-1/2" (14", 13-3/4") - 81 (78, 75) rows from beg, bind off 3 sts at beg of next 4 rows, bind off 2 sts at beg of next 4 rows = 86 (94, 102) sts.
Shape Neck: When back measures 9" (9-1/4", 9-3/4") from beg of armhole, bind off center 58 (62, 66) sts. Join 2nd ball of yarn to 2nd part and work at the same time. At each neck edge of every 2nd row,
bind off 2 sts once, dec 1 st once.
Shape Shoulders: When back measures 9-3/4" (10-1/4", 10-1/2") - 146 rows above ribbing, bind off rem 11 (13, 15) sts on each shoulder.

FRONT
Beg front same as back.
Shape Neck: When front measures 8-1/4" (8-1/2", 9") from beg of armhole, bind off center 52 (56, 60) sts. Join 2nd ball of yarn to 2nd part and work at the same time. At each neck edge of every 2nd row, bind off 3 sts once, bind off 2 sts once, dec 1 st once.
Shape Shoulders: When front measures 9-3/4" (10", 10-1/2") - 146 rows above ribbing, bind off rem 11 (13, 15) sts on each shoulder.

SLEEVE
With smaller size needles and MC, cast on 42 (46, 50) sts, work 1-1/2" in 1/1 ribbing. Purl 1 row on wrong side of work, inc 20 (18, 16) sts evenly spaced across row = 62 (64, 66) sts.
Change to larger size needles, work in St st. Inc 1 st each edge of every 8th row 12 (11, 10) times. Inc 1 st each edge of every 6th row 0 (2, 4) times. Work new sts in St st as you inc = 86 (90, 94) sts.
Shape Sleeve Top: When sleeve measures 17-1/2" from beg, bind off 3 sts at beg of next 8 (10, 12) rows, bind off 2 sts at beg of next 16 (12, 8) rows, bind off 3 sts at beg of next 6 (8, 10) rows, bind off rem 12 sts.

FINISHING
Embroider flower motif in duplicate stitch by foll chart, beg with 1 border st, then point 1 (2, 3) to point 4 (5, 6), 1 border st and in height from A to B. Use a single strand of yarn for embroidery. Center the chart on the sleeve. Sew shoulder seams. Neckband: With circular needle and MC, pick up and knit 158 (162, 166) sts around neck. Work 1" in 1/1 ribbing, bind off. Set in sleeves. Sew side and sleeve seams.

CHILD'S PULLOVER

SIZES
- 3 (5, 6) years
- Finished chest measurements: 26" (28", 30-1/2")
- Finished length: 14" (15-3/4", 18")
- Finished sleeve length: 9-3/4" (11", 12-1/4")

MATERIALS
- Neveda Valentine (50 g): 5 (6, 7) balls Light Rose - MC; 1 ball each Salmon - A, Yellow - B, Dark Rose - C, Green - D and Blue - E
- U.S. size 4 and 6 knitting needles. Circular needle U.S. size 4. (Metric sizes: 3.5, 4.0, and 3.5 circular.)

GAUGE
U.S. size 6 needles in St st: 4" (10 cm.) = 20 sts x 26 rows.
To save time, take time to check gauge!

BACK
With smaller size needles and MC, cast on 50 (54, 58) sts and work 1-1/2" in 1/1 ribbing. Purl 1 row on wrong side of work, inc 18 (20, 22) sts evenly spaced across row = 68 (74, 80) sts.
Change to larger size needles, work in St st.
Shape Armholes: When back measures 8-1/4" (9-1/4", 11-1/2") - 44 (52, 65) rows above ribbing, bind off 3 sts at beg of next 2 rows, bind off 2 sts at beg of next 2 rows = 58 (64, 70) sts.
Shape Neck: When back measures 5" (5-1/2", 6") from beg of armhole, bind off center 30 (32, 34) sts. Join 2nd ball of yarn to 2nd part and work at the same time. At each neck edge of every 2nd row, dec 1 st once.
Shape Shoulders: When back measures 6" (6-1/4", 6-1/2") - 83 (94, 109) rows above ribbing, bind off rem 13 (15, 17) sts on each shoulder.

FRONT
Beg front same as back.
Shape Neck: When front measures 4-3/4" (5", 5-1/4") from beg of armhole, bind off center 24 (26, 28) sts. Join 2nd ball of yarn to 2nd part and work at the same time. At each neck edge of every 2nd row, bind off 2 sts once, dec 1 st twice.
Shape Shoulders: When front measures 6" (6-1/4", 6-1/2") - 83 (94, 109) rows above ribbing, bind off rem 13 (15, 17) sts on each shoulder.

SLEEVE
With smaller size needles and MC, cast on 30 (34, 38) sts, work 1-1/4" in 1/1 ribbing. Purl 1 row on wrong side of work, inc 20 (18, 16) sts evenly spaced across row = 50 (52, 54) sts.
Change to larger size needles, work in St st. Inc 1 st each edge of every 14th (13th, 12th) row 4 (5, 6) times. Work new sts in St st as you inc = 58 (62, 66) sts.
Shape Sleeve Top: When sleeve measures 9-3/4" (11", 12-1/4") from beg, bind off 4 sts at beg of next 12 rows, bind off rem 10 (14, 18) sts.

FINISHING
Embroider motif in duplicate stitch by foll chart, beg with 1 border st and point 1 (2, 3) to point 4 (5, 6), 1 border st and in height from point A (B, C) to D (E, F). Center chart on sleeves. Sew shoulder seams. With circular needle and double strand of MC, pick up and knit 78 (80, 82) sts around neck.

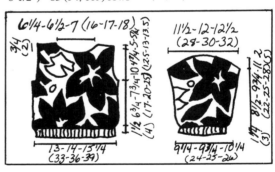

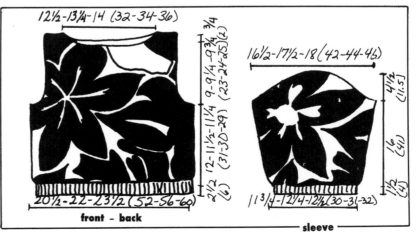

front - back

sleeve

CHILD'S PULLOVER

Work 1" in 1/1 ribbing,
bind off.
Sew sleeves to side seams,
matching center of sleeve
to shoulder seam. Sew side
and sleeve seams.

KEY TO CHART
2 dark rose
3 yellow
5 salmon
1 blue
4 green

KEY TO CHART
5 salmon
3 yellow
2 dark rose
4 green
1 blue

WOMAN'S PULLOVER

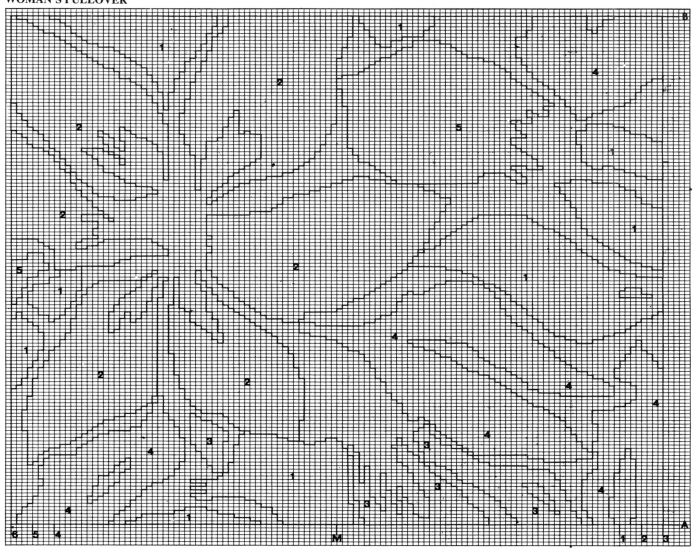

FRESH

FRESH

Alternating bands

of check stitches and

embroidered flower motifs

create a fresh design.

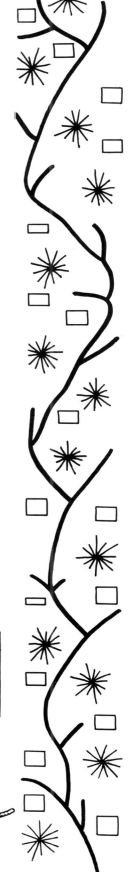

SIZES
■ Small (Medium, Large)
■ Finished measurements above ribbing: 38-1/2" (40", 43")
■ Finished length: 19-3/4"
■ Finished sleeve length: 7" (7-1/4", 7-3/4")

MATERIALS
■ Mayflower Cotton 8 (50 g): 6 (7, 7) balls White - MC; 2 (2, 3) balls Light Blue - A; 1 ball Yellow - B
■ DMC embroidery floss: green-704 and rose-893
■ U.S. size 2 and 3 knitting needles. 24" Circular needle U.S. size 2. (Metric sizes: 2.5, 3.0, and 2.5 60 cm. circular.)

GAUGE
U.S. size 3 needles in St st: 4" (10 cm.) = 26 sts x 36 rows.
U.S. size 3 needles in check St st: 4" = 30 sts x 36 rows.
To save time, take time to check gauge!

BACK
With smaller size needles and MC, cast on 110 (114, 122) sts and work 2" in 1/1 ribbing. Purl 1 row on wrong side of work row, inc 29 (30, 32) sts evenly spaced across row = 139 (144, 154) sts.
Change to larger size needles, work as foll: 1 border st, 6 sts in check pattern by foll chart 1, beg at point A, *13 (14, 16) sts in MC, 15 sts in check st* , work * to * 4 times total, 13 (14, 16) sts in MC, 6 sts in check st, 1 border st. Carry unused yarn loosely across wrong side of work row for check st. Do not carry blue yarn across white sections. Inc 1 st at each edge of every 4th row 8 (6, 2) times. Inc 1 st at each edge of every 2nd row 29 (32, 38) times = 213 (220, 234) sts. Work inc sts as foll: 9 sts in check st, 13 (14, 16) sts in MC, 15 sts in check st.
Shape Neck: When back

measures 18-3/4" from beg, bind off center 51 (54, 60) sts. Join 2nd ball of yarn to 2nd part and work at the same time. At each neck edge of every 2nd row, bind off 8 sts twice, bind off 4 sts once.
Shape Shoulders: When back measures 19-3/4" from beg, end with 2nd row of check st, bind off rem 61 (63, 67) sts on each shoulder.

FRONT
Beg front same as back.
Shape Neck: When front measures 17-3/4" from beg, bind off center 43 (46, 52) sts. Join 2nd ball of yarn to 2nd part and work at the same time. At each neck edge of every 2nd row, bind off 6 sts once, bind off 4 sts twice, bind off 3 sts twice, bind off 2 sts twice.
Shape Shoulders: When front measures 19-3/4" from beg, end with 2 rows of check st, bind off rem 61 (63, 67) sts on each shoulder.

FINISHING
Sew shoulder seams. Embroider pieces using sketch and photo as a guide. Em-

broider stems in chain st in green and embroider over shoulder seams. Embroider flowers in star stitch. Embroider yellow rectangles in duplicate stitch. With circular needle and MC, pick up and knit 174 (180, 186) sts around neck.
Work 2" in 1/1 ribbing, dec 1 st at each shoulder seam by k2 tog at right shoulder seam and sl 1, k1, psso left shoulder seam. Bind off.
Sleeve Cuffs: With smaller size needles and MC, pick up and knit 76 (80, 84) sts from sleeve end and work 2" in 1/1 ribbing. Bind off loosely. Sew side and sleeve seams.

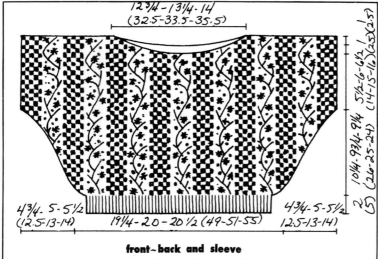

12 3/4 - 13 1/4 - 14
(32.5-33.5-35.5)

5 1/2 - 6 - 6 1/2 (14-15-16)

2 (5)

10 1/4 - 9 3/4 - 9 1/4 (26-25-24)

10 (25) (2.5)

4 3/4 · 5 · 5 1/2 (12.5-13-14)

19 1/4 - 20 - 20 1/2 (49-51-55)

4 3/4 · 5 · 5 1/2 (12.5-13-14)

front~back and sleeve

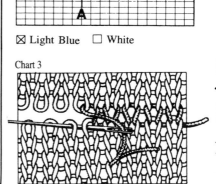

Chart 1

⊠ Light Blue   ☐ White

Chart 3

TROPICAL

TROPICAL

Bright tropical colors and large palm motifs create beautiful lookalike sweaters for mother and daughter.

WOMAN'S PULLOVER

SIZES

■ Small (Medium, Large)
■ Finished bust measurements: 42-1/2" (45", 47")
■ Finished length: 21-1/4"
■ Finished sleeve length: 1-3/4"

MATERIALS

■ Neveda Valentine: (50 g): 6 balls Yellow - MC; 3 balls Green - A; 1 ball each Orange - B, White - C, Rose - D and Black - E
■ U.S. size 4 and 6 knitting needles. 16" Circular needle U.S. size 4. (Metric sizes: 3.5, 4.0, and 3.5 40 cm. circular.)

GAUGE

U.S. size 6 needles in St st: 4" (10 cm.) = 20 sts x 30 rows.
To save time, take time to check gauge!

BACK

With smaller size needles and MC, cast on 94 (98, 102) sts and work 1-1/2" in 1/1 ribbing. Purl 1 row on wrong side of work, inc 16 (18, 20) sts evenly spaced across row = 110 (116, 122) sts.
Change to larger size needles, work in St st foll chart. Beg with 1 border st, then point S (M, L) and end with point S1 (M1, L1) on chart, 1 border st. Use a separate ball of yarn for each section of color. Be sure to cross yarns on wrong side of work when changing colors.
Shape Sleeves: When back measures 11-1/2" (11",10-1/2") from beg, inc 1 st each edge of every 2nd row 5 times = 120 (126, 132) sts.
Shape Neck: When back measures 20-3/4" from beg, bind off center 44 (46, 48) sts. Join 2nd ball of yarn to 2nd part and work at the same time. At each neck edge of every 2nd row, bind off 10 sts once.
Shape Shoulders: When back measures 21-1/4" from beg, bind off rem 28 (30, 32) sts on each shoulder.

FRONT

Beg front same as back.
Shape Neck: When front measures 20" from beg, bind off center 24 (26, 28) sts. Join 2nd ball of yarn to 2nd part and work at the same time. At each neck edge of every 2nd row, bind off 8 sts once, bind off 6 sts once, bind off 4 sts once, bind off 2 sts once.
Shape Shoulders: When front measures 21-1/4" from beg, bind off rem 28 (30, 32) sts on each shoulder.

FINISHING

Embroider the black lines in duplicate stitch by foll chart. Sew shoulder seams.
Neckband: With circular needle and MC, pick up and knit 134 (138, 142) sts around neck. Work 3/4" in 1/1 ribbing, bind off.
Sleevebands: With smaller size needles and MC, pick up and knit 122 (126, 130) sts along sleeve and work 3/4" in 1/1 ribbing, bind off.
Sew side and sleeve seams.

CHILD'S PULLOVER

SIZES

■ 6 (12, 24) Months
■ Finished chest measurements: 24-1/2" (25", 26")
■ Finished length: 11" (12-1/4", 13")
■ Finished sleeve length: 8-1/2" (9", 9-1/2")

MATERIALS

■ Neveda Valentine (50 g): 3 balls Yellow - MC; 2 balls Green - A; 1 ball each White - B, Rose - C and Black - D
■ U.S. size 4 and 6 knitting needles. (Metric sizes: 3.5 and 4.0.) 6 buttons.

GAUGE

U.S. size 6 needles in St st: 4" (10 cm.) = 20 sts x 30 rows.
To save time, take time to check gauge!

BACK

With smaller size needles and MC, cast on 52 (56, 60) sts and work 1-1/2" in 1/1 ribbing. Purl 1 row on wrong side of work, inc 12 (10, 8) sts evenly spaced across row = 64 (66, 68) sts.
Change to larger size needles, work in St st foll chart. Beg with 1 border st, point 1 (2, 3) and end with point 4 (5, 6) on chart, 1 border st. Use a separate ball of yarn for each section of color. Be sure to cross yarns on wrong side of work when changing colors.
Shape Neck: When back measures 10-1/4" (11-1/2", 12-1/4") from beg, bind off center 16 (16, 18) sts. Join 2nd ball of yarn to 2nd part and work at the same time. At each neck edge of every 2nd row, bind off 5 sts once.
Work to last row of chart. Change to smaller size needles and MC and knit 1 row on right side of work. Work 1/4" in 1/1 ribbing, then make 2 buttonholes on each shoulder. Work 5 (6, 6) sts, bind off 3 sts, work 4 sts, bind off 3 sts, work 4 sts. On foll row, cast on 3 sts over bound off sts of previous row. When border measures 3/4", bind off rem 19 (20, 20) sts on each shoulder.

FRONT

Beg front same as back.
Shape Neck: When front measures 9-1/4" (10-1/2", 11-1/2") from beg, bind off center 8 (8, 10) sts. Join 2nd ball of yarn to 2nd part and work at the same time. At each neck edge of every 2nd row, bind off 5 sts once, bind off 3 sts once, dec 1 st once.
Change to smaller size needles and MC and knit 1 row on right side of work. Work 3/4" in 1/1 ribbing,

WOMAN'S PULLOVER

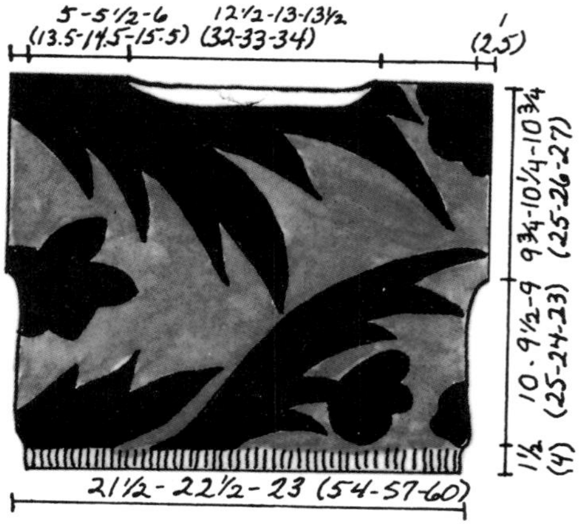
5-5½-6
(13.5-14.5-15.5)
12½-13-13½
(32-33-34)
1
(2.5)
9¾-10¼-10¾
(25-26-27)
10-9½-9
(25-24-23)
1½
(4)
21½-22½-23 (54-57-60)

CHILD'S PULLOVER

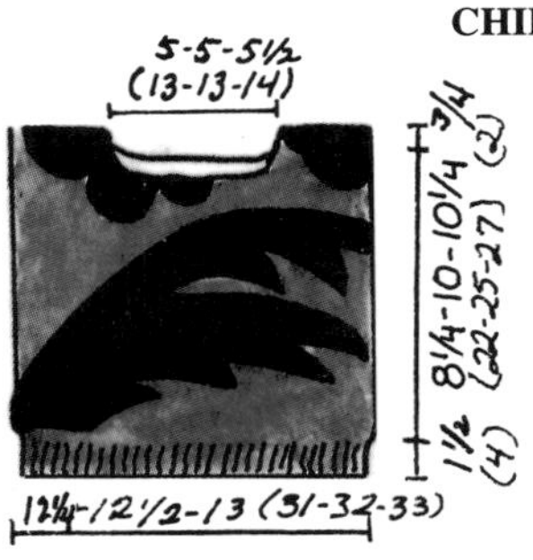
5-5-5½
(13-13-14)
¾
(2)
8¼-10-10¼
(22-25-27)
1½
(4)
12¼-12½-13 (31-32-33)

front – back

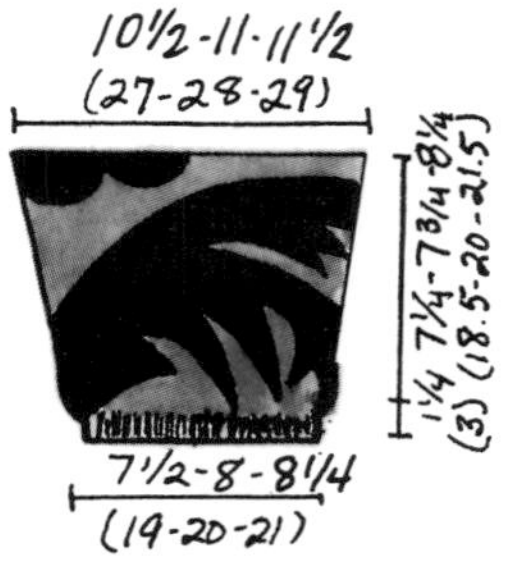
10½-11-11½
(27-28-29)
7¼-7¾-8¼
(18.5-20-21.5)
1¼
(3)
7½-8-8¼
(19-20-21)

sleeve

bind off rem 19 (20, 20) sts on each shoulder.

SLEEVES

With smaller size needles and MC, cast on 26 (30, 34) sts and work 1-1/4" in 1/1 ribbing. Purl 1 row on wrong side of work, inc 14 (12, 10) sts evenly spaced across row = 40 (42, 44) sts.
Change to larger size needles and work in St st centering chart at point M. Inc 1 st each edge of every 6th (7th, 7th) row 8 times. Work new sts in St st as you inc = 56 (58, 60) sts. When sleeve measures 8-1/2" (9", 9-1/2") from beg, bind off all sts.

FINISHING

Embroider black lines in duplicate stitch by foll chart. Neckband: With smaller size needles and MC, pick up and knit 35 (35, 37) sts along back neck. Work 3/4" in 1/1 ribbing, bind off. With smaller size needles and MC, pick up and knit 41 (41, 43) sts along front neck. Work 3/4" in 1/1 ribbing, but when border measures 1/4" from beg, make 1 buttonhole 3 sts from edge, bind off 3 sts. On foll row, cast on 3 sts over bound off sts. When band measures 3/4" from beg, bind off.
Sew sleeves to side seams,

matching center of sleeve with shoulder seam. Sew side and sleeve seams. Reinforce buttonholes and sew on buttons.

KEY TO CHART

⊡ or 1 = MC
2 = A
⊡ = B
3 = C
⊡ = D

CHILD'S PULLOVER

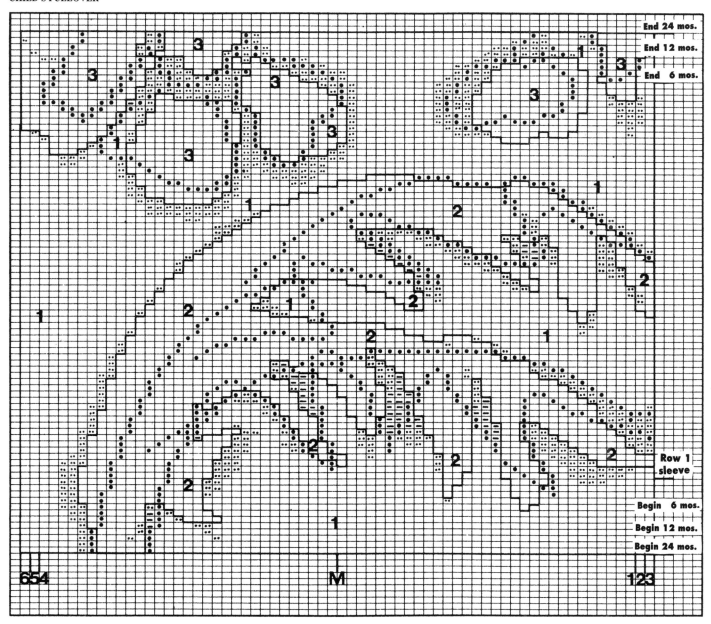

KEY TO CHART

☒ or 1 = MC
         2 = A
☑ or 3 = B
⊡ = C
⊟ or 4 = D
⊡ = E

(Top)

Row 1

S M L

WOMAN'S PULLOVER

28

BOUQUET

✿ BOUQUET

Knitted bobbles and crocheted

petals combine to create a

bouquet of fresh daisies.

SIZES
- Small (Medium, Large)
- Finished bust measurements: 41" (43", 45-1/2")
- Finished length: 18"
- Finished sleeve length: 9-3/4"

MATERIALS
- Mayflower Cotton 8 (50 g): 9 (9, 10) balls Green - MC; 2 balls each Yellow - A and White - B
- U.S. size 2 and 3 knitting needles. 29" Circular needle U.S. size 2. Crochet Hook U.S. size B/1. (Metric sizes: 2.5, 3.0, and 2.5 circular; 2.5 crochet hook.)

GAUGE
U.S. size 3 needles in St st: 4" (10 cm.) = 26 sts x 36 rows.
To save time, take time to check gauge!

BACK
With smaller size needles and MC, cast on 126 (130, 134) sts and work 3/4" in 1/1 ribbing. Purl 1 row on wrong side of work, inc 11 (15, 19) sts evenly spaced across row = 137 (145, 153) sts.
Change to larger size needles, work in St st.
Shape Armholes: When back measures 9" (8-1/2", 8-1/4") from beg-76 (72, 68) rows above ribbing, bind off 3 sts at beg of next 4 rows. Bind off 2 sts at beg of next 4 rows. Dec 1 st at each edge of every 2nd row 3 times = 111 (119, 127) sts.
When back measures 5-1/2" (6", 6-1/4") above armhole shaping, 126 rows above ribbing, work in bobbles by centering chart 1 at point M1 (M2, M3). For each bobble, join 16" of A. In 1 st, k5 alternately in

front and back of st, turn, p5, turn, k5, turn, p5, turn, slip the last 4 sts one after another over the first st.
Shape Neck: When back measures 8-1/4" (8-1/2", 9") above armhole shaping - 151 rows above ribbing, bind off center 57 (59, 61) sts. Join 2nd ball of yarn to 2nd part and work at the same time. At each neck edge of every 2nd row, bind off 4 sts once, bind off 2 sts once. Shape Shoulders: When back measures 17-1/4" from beg, at each armhole edge of every 2nd row, bind off 11 (12, 14) sts 1 (2, 1) time, bind off 10 (0, 13) sts once.

FRONT
Beg front same as back. When front measures 3-1/4" from beg 24 rows above ribbing, work by centering chart 2 at point M1 (M2, M3). Shape armholes as on back.
Shape Neck: When front measures 7" (7-1/2", 8") from beg of armhole -141 rows above ribbing, bind off center 25 (27, 29) sts. Join 2nd ball of yarn to 2nd part and work at the same time. At each neck edge of every 2nd row, bind off 6 sts once, bind off 4 sts twice, bind off 3 sts once, bind off 2 sts twice, dec 1 st once.
Shape Shoulders: When front measures 17-1/4" from beg, shape shoulders as on back.

SLEEVE
With smaller size needles and MC, cast on 76 (78, 80) sts, work 3/4" in 1/1 ribbing. Purl 1 row on wrong side of work row, inc 10 sts evenly spaced across row = 86 (88, 90) sts.

Change to larger size needles, work in St st. Inc 1 st each edge of every 6th (6th, 4th) row 5 (12, 6) times. Inc 1 st each edge of every 8th (8th, 6th) row 6 (1, 9) times = 108 (114, 120) sts. Work new sts in St st as you inc.
When sleeve measures 9-3/4" from beg, work by centering chart 3. **At the same time,**
Shape Sleeve Top: Bind off 3 sts at beg of next 6 rows. Bind off 2 sts at beg of next 26 rows. Bind off 3 sts at beg of next 4 rows. Bind off 3 (4, 5) sts at beg of next 2 rows. Bind off 4 (5, 6) sts at beg of next 2 rows. Bind off rem 12 (14, 16) sts.

FINISHING
Join an 8" strand of B to each bobble and make a chain with crochet hook. Thread end in tapestry needle and sew to bobble as shown in photo. Sew shoulder seams. With circular needle and MC, pick up and knit 134 (138, 142) sts around neck. Work 3/4" in 1/1 ribbing, bind off. Set in sleeves, matching center of sleeve to shoulder seam. Sew side and sleeve seams.

KEY TO CHARTS
- ☐ St st(knit right side of work rows, purl wrong side of work rows) - MC
- ⊡ Bobble - A

Chart 3

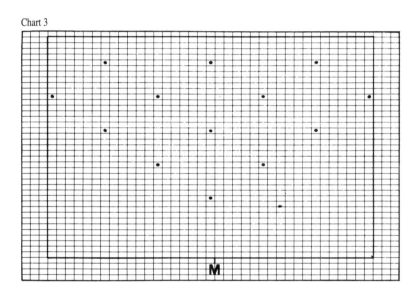

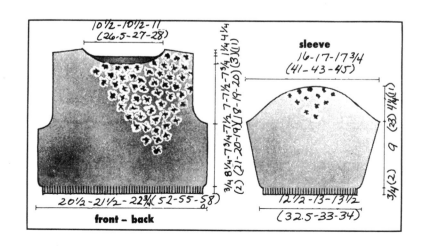

10½-10½-11
(26.5-27-28)

20½-21½-22¾(52-55-58)

front – back

8¼-8¼-7½-7¼-7¾-7½-7¾ (3)(11)
¾ (21-20-19)(18-19-20)
¾ (2)
(2) 4¼ (11)

sleeve
16-17-17¾
(41-43-45)

12½-13-13½
(32.5-33-34)
9 (23) ¾(2)

Chart 1

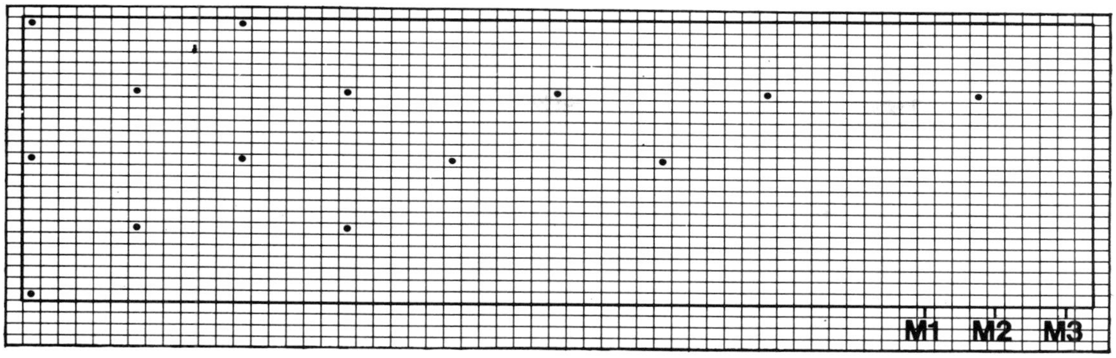

M1 M2 M3

Chart 2

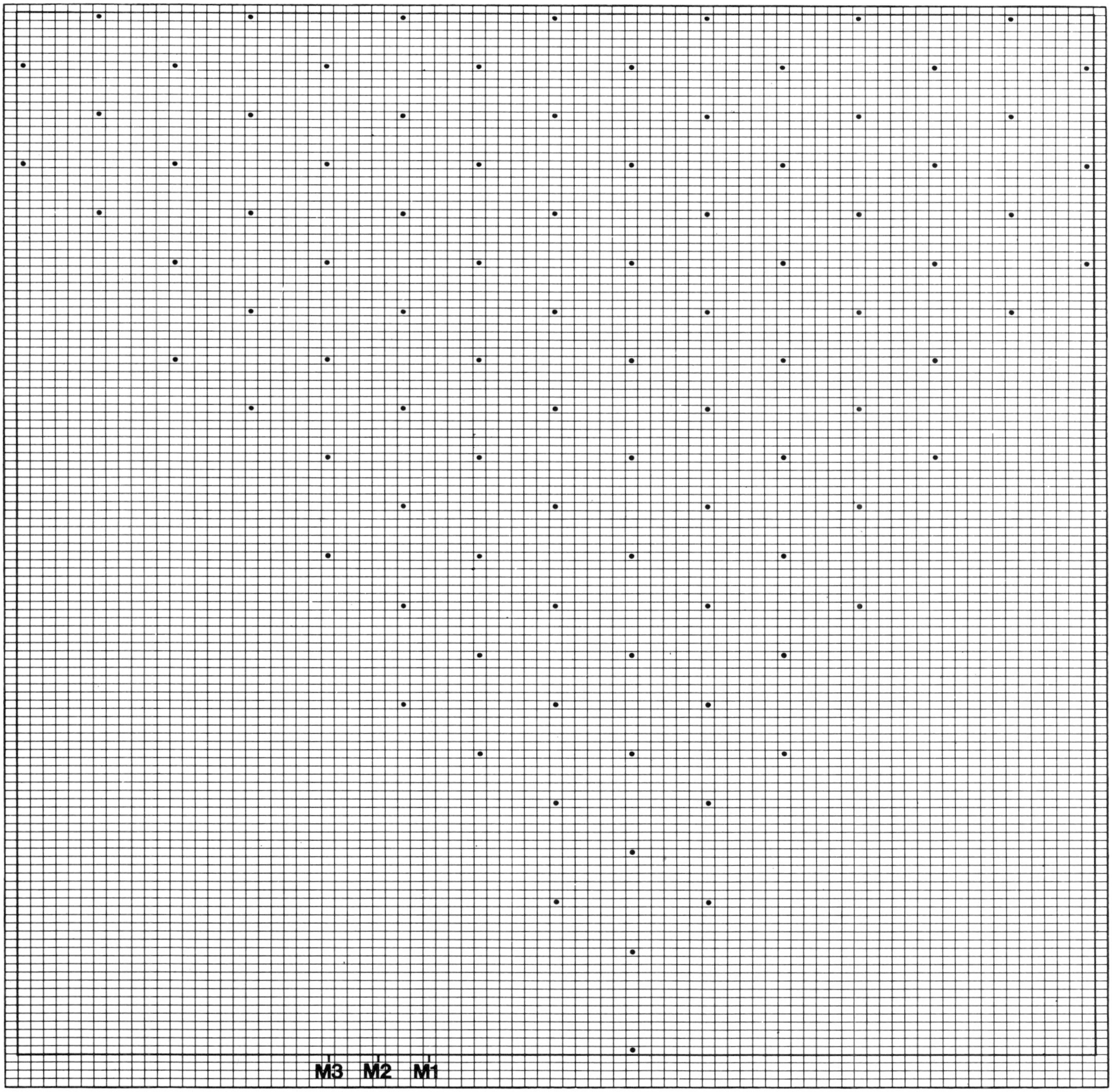

M3 M2 M1

KEY TO CHART
2 = MC
1 = CC

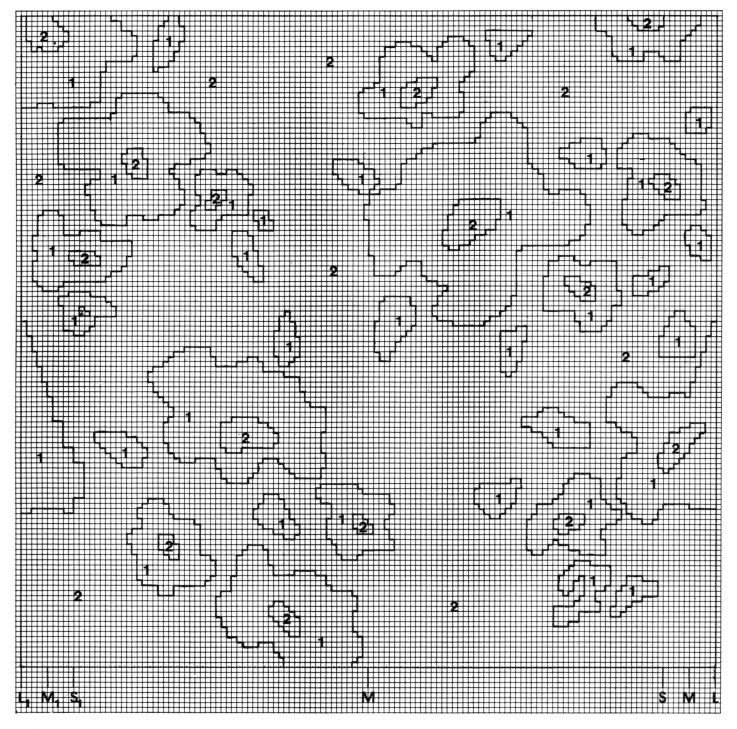

❀ NATURAL

Large white flowers on a

pale blue background echo

the clouds of a summer sky.

SIZES
- Small (Medium, Large)
- Finished bust measurements: 40" (43-1/2", 47")
- Finished length: 24"
- Finished sleeve length: 17-1/4"

MATERIALS
- Mayflower Felina (50 g): 10 (10, 11) balls Blue - MC; 4 (5, 5) balls White - CC
- U.S. size 4 and 6 knitting needles. Circular needle U.S. size 4. (Metric sizes: 3.5, 4.0, and 3.5 circular.)

GAUGE
U.S. size 6 needles in St st: 4" (10 cm.) = 22 sts x 26 rows.
U.S. size 6 needles in intarsia St st: 4" = 21 sts x 26 rows.
To save time, take time to check gauge!

BACK
With smaller size needles and MC, cast on 94 (102, 106) sts and work 3-1/4" in 2/2 ribbing, beg with 1 border st, *k2, p2*, rep * to *, end with 1 border st. Purl 1 row on wrong side of work, inc 20 (22, 28) sts evenly spaced across row = 114 (124, 134) sts. Change to larger size needles, work in intarsia St st foll chart. Beg at point S (M, L) and end at point S1 (M1, L1). Use a separate ball of yarn for each section of color. Be sure to cross yarns on wrong side of work when changing colors. If you desire, you can embroider small motifs in duplicate stitch on finished work.
When back measures about 22-1/2" from beg—last row of chart, work 1-1/2" in 2/2 ribbing. Bind off loosely.

FRONT
Work front same as back.

SLEEVE
With smaller size needles and MC, cast on 42 (46, 46) sts, work 2-1/2" in 2/2 ribbing. Purl 1 row on wrong side of work, inc 22 (22, 26) sts evenly spaced across row = 64 (68, 72) sts.
Change to larger size needles, work in intarsia St st centering chart. Inc 1 st each edge of every 4th row 16 (15, 14) times. Inc 1 st each edge of every 2nd row 12 (14, 15) times. Work new sts in intarsia St st as you inc = 120 (126, 130) sts.
When sleeve measures 17-1/4" from beg, bind off all sts.

FINISHING
Embroider small motifs in CC in duplicate stitch. Sew shoulder seams over 5" (5-1/2", 6-1/4") at each edge. Sew sleeves to side seams, matching center of sleeve to shoulder seam. Sew side and sleeve seams.

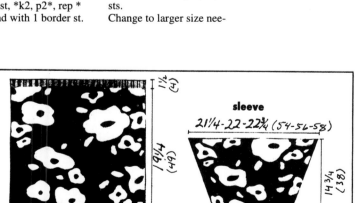

❀ DELICATE

Delicate roses were

embroidered onto a

soft summer sweater.

SIZES
- Small (Medium, Large)
- Finished bust measurements: 39-1/2" (43", 45-1/2")
- Finished length: 20"

MATERIALS
- Mayflower Cotton 8 (50 g): 6 (7, 7) balls Aqua
- DMC Embroidery floss: dark rose-335, green-502, light green-504, beige-712, light moss green-772, rose-893, light salmon-948, light pink-963, moss green-3347, medium moss green-3348, peach-3706, light rose-3708 and white.
- U.S. size 2 and 3 knitting needles. 16" Circular needle U.S. size 2. (Metric sizes: 2.5, 3.0, and 2.5 40 cm. circular.)

GAUGE
U.S. size 3 needles in St st: 4" (10 cm.) = 26 sts x 32 rows.
To save time, take time to check gauge!

- **Long stitch: Row 1:** right side facing, 1 border st, *k1 by wrapping yarn around needle twice*, rep * to *, 1 border st. **Row 2:** Purl 1 in each stitch, dropping the extra wrapped yarn.
- **Eyelet stitch: Rows 1 to 4:** St st. **Row 5:** 1 border st, k7 (7, 1), *k2 tog, yo, k10*, rep * to * across, end with k2 tog, yo, k7 (1, 7), 1 border st.
Rows 6 to 10: St st. **Row 11:** 1 border st, *k4, k2 tog, yo*, rep * to * across, end with k4, 1 border st. **Rows 12 to 16:** St st. **Row 17:** 1 border st, k1 (1, 7), *k2 tog, yo, k10*, rep * to *, end with k2 tog, yo, k1 (7, 1), 1 border st. **Rows 18 to 20:** St st.

BACK
With smaller size needles and Aqua, cast on 128 (138, 148) sts and work 1-1/4" in 1/1 ribbing.
Change to larger size needles, work as foll: 1-1/2" in St st, 2 rows of long stitch, 7" (6-1/2", 6-1/2") in St st, 2 rows of long stitch, 6-1/2" (7", 7") of St st, 2 rows of long stitch, 2-1/2" of eyelet pattern. **At the same time,**
Shape Sleeves: When back

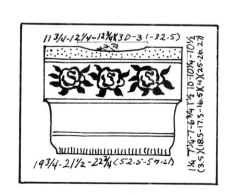

measures 8-1/2" (8-1/4", 8") from beg, at each edge of every 2nd row, cast on 1 st 3 (5, 4) times, cast on 2 sts 4(2,3) times = 150 (156, 168) sts.
Shape Neck: When back measures 19-1/4" from beg, bind off center 44 (46, 50) sts. Join 2nd ball of yarn to 2nd part and work at the same time. At each neck edge of every 2nd row, bind off 7 sts once, bind off 4 sts once, bind off 3 sts once.
Shape Shoulders: When back measures 20" from beg, bind off rem 39 (41, 45) sts on each shoulder.

FRONT

Beg front same as back.
Shape Neck: When front measures 18" from beg, bind off center 24 (26, 30) sts. Join 2nd ball of yarn to 2nd part and work at the same time. At each neck edge of every 2nd row, bind off 7 sts once, bind off 4 sts once, bind off 3 sts once, bind off 2 sts 5 times.
Shape Shoulders: When

front measures 20" from beg, bind off rem 39 (41, 45) sts on each shoulder.

NECKBAND

Sew shoulder seams. With circular needle and Aqua, pick up and knit 134 (138, 144) sts around neck. Work 3/4" in 1/1 ribbing, bind off.

FINISHING

Embroider front by foll chart on upper band of St st. Beg on the 2nd (5th, 5th) row above long stitch rows and center the chart. Use 3 strands of embroidery floss and work in duplicate stitch. Embroider the black lines by foll chart in stem stitch in dark rose. With light rose, embroider in hem stitch along upper and lower edges of long stitch rows on back and front. Armbands: With circular needle and Aqua, pick up and knit 126 (130, 134) sts along sleeve edge and work 3/4" in 1/1 ribbing. Bind off loosely. Sew side and sleeve seams.

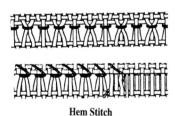

Hem Stitch

KEY TO CHART

- ◪ green
- ◱ light green
- ⊡ beige
- ◿ light moss green
- ◵ light salmon
- ◉ moss green-3347
- ⊠ medium moss green-3348
- ⊠ peach-3706
- ◲ light rose-3708
- ⊡ white
- ◺

36

DESIGNER

A casual sweater embellished with colorful cascading leaves makes a designer impression.

SIZES
■ Small (Medium, Large)
■ Finished bust measurements: 41-1/2" (44-1/2", 47")
■ Finished length: 26" (26-1/2", 26-3/4")

MATERIALS
■ Scheepjeswol Domino or Mayflower Felina (50 g): 6 (7, 8) balls Salmon - MC; 3 balls Yellow - A; 1 ball each Dark Green - B and Khaki - C
■ U.S. size 3 and 5 knitting needles. 16" Circular needle U.S. size 3. (Metric sizes: 3.0, 3.75, and 3.0 40 cm. circular.)

GAUGE
U.S. size 5 needles in St st: 4" (10 cm.) = 22 sts x 31 rows.
To save time, take time to check gauge!

BACK
With smaller size needles and A, cast on 100 (108, 114) sts and work 2" (2-1/2", 2-3/4") in 1/1 ribbing. Purl 1 row on wrong side of work, inc 18 (18, 20) sts evenly spaced across row = 118 (126, 134) sts.
Change to larger size needles, work in St st.
Shape Armholes: When back measures 17" - 118 (115, 122) rows above ribbing, bind off 3 sts at beg of next 2 rows. Bind off 2 sts at beg of next 2 rows. Dec 1 st at each edge of every 2nd row once = 106 (114, 122) sts.
Shape Neck: When armhole measures 8-1/4" (8-3/4", 9") - 183 rows above ribbing, bind off center 48 (52, 56) sts. Join 2nd ball

of yarn to 2nd part and work at the same time. At each neck edge of every 2nd row, bind off 3 sts once, bind off 2 sts once.
At the same time, Shape Shoulders: At armhole edge of every 2nd row, bind off 8 (8, 9) sts 3 (1, 2) times, bind off 0 (9, 10) sts 0 (2, 1) time.

FRONT
Beg front same as back, but work by foll chart above ribbing, beg with 1 border st, then work from point 1 (2, 3) to point 4 (5,

6), end with 1 border st. Use a separate ball of yarn for each section of color. Be sure to cross yarn on wrong side of work when changing colors. Embroider small motifs later in duplicate stitch. Shape armholes as on back = 106 (114, 122) sts.
Shape Neck: When front measures 23" (23-1/2", 23-3/4") above ribbing-point D on chart, bind off center 34 (38, 42) sts. Join 2nd ball of yarn to 2nd part and work at the same time. At each neck edge of every 2nd row, bind off 3 sts once, bind off 2 sts twice, dec 1 st 5 times.
Shape shoulder at point E on chart same as on back.

FINISHING
Embroider the smaller motifs in duplicate stitch by following chart. Sew shoulder seams. With circular needle and MC, pick up and knit 142 (150, 158) sts around neck. Work 2" in 1/1 ribbing as foll: 4

rounds in B, 4 rounds in C, complete in MC, bind off. Sew side seams. With circular needle and MC, pick up and knit 90 (94, 98) sts around armhole. Work 1-1/4" in 1/1 ribbing. Bind off loosely.

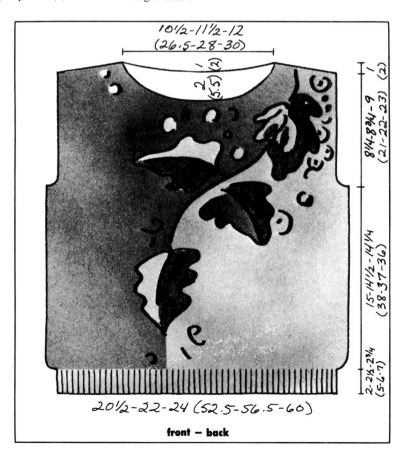

10½-11½-12
(26.5-28-30)

2 (5.5)

1 (2)

8¼-8¾-9
(21-22-23)

1 (2)

15-14½-14¼
(38-37-36)

2-2⅓-2¾
(5-6-7)

20½-22-24 (52.5-56.5-60)

front – back

KEY TO CHART
- • = B
- 7 = MC
- V or 8 = A
- X or 9 = C

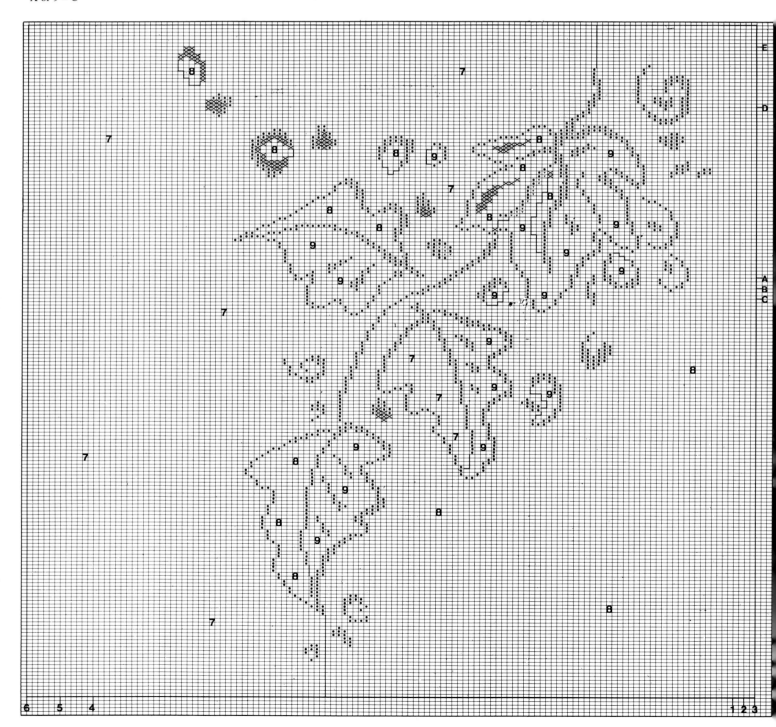

CREATIVE

A loose-fitting crop top with colorful vertical stripes is embroidered with flowers, foliage, and creative tendrils.

SIZES
■ Small (Medium, Large)
■ Finished bust measurements: 44" (45-1/2", 47")
■ Finished length: 19-1/4"
■ Finished sleeve length: 9-3/4"

MATERIALS
■ Mayflower Felina (50 g): 5 balls White - MC; 3 balls each Blue - A and Lilac - B; 2 balls Black - C
■ U.S. size 3 and 5 knitting needles. 16" Circular needle U.S. size 3. (Metric sizes: 3.0, 3.75, and 3.0 40 cm. circular.)

GAUGE
U.S. size 5 needles in St st: 4" (10 cm.) = 21 sts x 31 rows.
To save time, take time to check gauge!

FRONT
With smaller size needles and MC, cast on 120 (124, 128) sts and work 1" in 1/1 ribbing.
Change to larger size needles, work in St st foll chart 1. Work 1 border st, then work from point 1 (2, 3) to point 4 (5, 6), end with 1 border st. Use a separate ball of yarn to each section of color. Be sure to cross yarns on wrong side of work when changing colors. Embroider the black motif in duplicate stitch on finished work.
Shape Armholes: When front measures 11-1/2" (11", 10-1/2") from beg - point C (B, A) on chart, bind off 2 sts at beg of next 2 rows. Dec 1 st at each edge of every 2nd row twice = 112 (116 ,120) sts.
Shape Neck: When front measures 6-1/4" (6-1/2", 7") from beg of armhole-point D on chart, bind off center 10 (12 ,14) sts. Join 2nd ball of yarn to 2nd part and work at the same time. At each neck edge of every 2nd row, bind off 3 sts twice, bind off 2 sts 3 times, dec 1 st 4 times.
Shape Shoulders: When front measures 8-1/4" (8-1/2", 9") from beg of armhole-point E on chart, bind off 12 sts at beg of next 4 (6, 4) rows. Bind off 11 (0, 13) sts at beg of next 2 rows.

BACK
Beg back same as front, rev chart so that you work 1 border st, point 4 (5, 6) to point 1 (2, 3), 1 border st. Shape Armholes as on front.
Shape Neck: When back measures 8-1/4" (8-1/2", 9") from beg-point E on chart, bind off center 34 (36, 38) sts. Join 2nd ball of yarn to 2nd part and work at the same time. At each neck edge of every 2nd row, bind off 4 sts once. **At the same time**, Shape shoulders as on front.

LEFT SLEEVE
With smaller size needles and MC, cast on 80 (82, 84) sts, work 1" in 1/1 ribbing.
Change to larger size needles, work in St st foll chart. Work 1 border st, then from point 1 (2, 3) to point 4 (5 ,6), end with 1 border st. When chart is complete, continue in St st in A. Inc 1 st each edge of every 6th row 2 (5, 7) times. Inc 1 st each edge of every 10th row 5 (3, 2) times. Work new sts in St st as you inc = 94 (98, 102) sts.
When sleeve measures 9-3/4" from beg, end wrong side of work row.
Shape Sleeve Top: Bind off 4 sts at beg of next 6 rows. Bind off 6 sts at beg of next 2 rows. Bind off 7 sts at beg of next 2 rows. Bind off 9 sts at beg of next 2 rows. Bind off rem 26 (30, 34) sts.

RIGHT SLEEVE
Work same as left sleeve, but reverse chart: 1 border st, then point 4 (5, 6) to point 1 (2, 3), 1 border st, complete in B.

FINISHING
Emboider the black motifs on the white bands on body and sleeves by foll chart. Sew shoulder seams. With circular needle and A, pick up and knit 88 (92, 96) sts around neck. Work 2" in 1/1 ribbing, bind off. Fold to inside and slip stitch in place. Set in sleeves, matching center of sleeve to shoulder seams. Sew side and sleeve seams. Fold lower 1" on body and sleeves to inside and slip stitch in place.

Chart 2

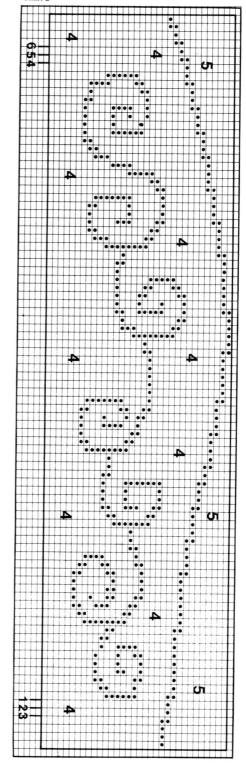

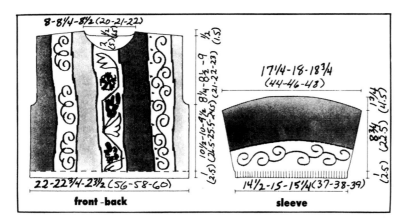

front -back

sleeve

(Top)

KEY TO CHART
4 = MC
5 = A
6 = B
⊡ = C

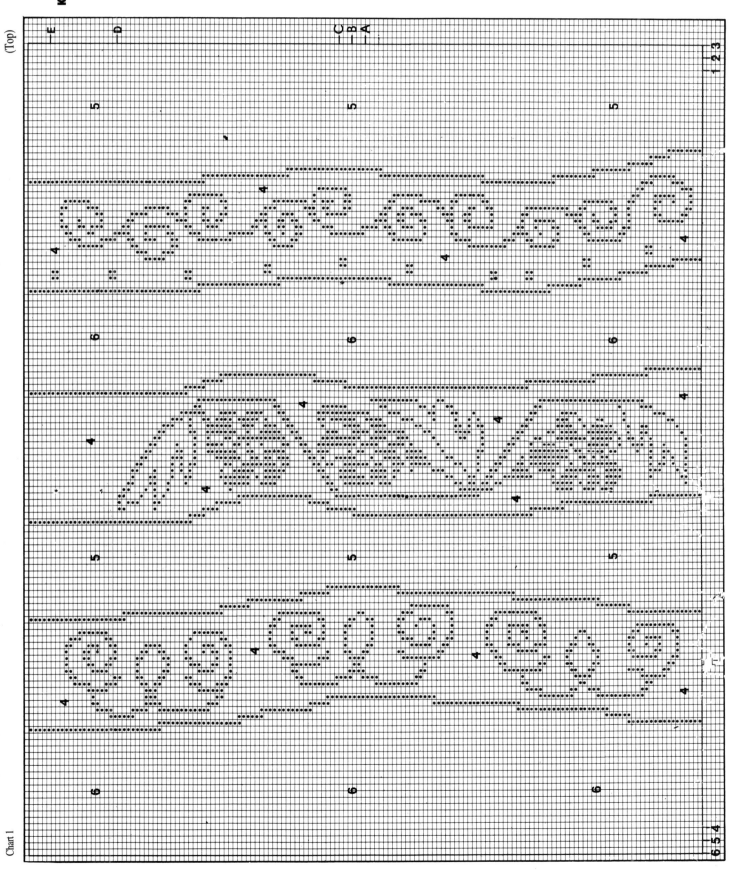

Chart 1

43

PLAYFUL

⚘ PLAYFUL

Embellish this playful

striped sweater with

embroidered flowers

scattered as you like.

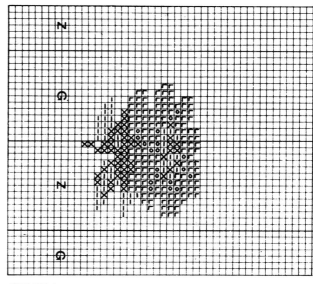

CHART 1

SIZES
■ Small (Medium, Large)
■ Finished bust measurements: 44" (46", 47")
■ Finished length: 21-1/2"
■ Finished sleeve length: 13-1/4" (13-1/4", 14")

MATERIALS
■ Mayflower Helarsgarn (50 g): 7 (8, 8) balls Turquoise - MC; 6 (7, 7) balls Light Turquoise - A; 1 ball each Red - B, Pink - C, Dark Blue - D and Blue - E
■ U.S. size 4 and 6 knitting needles. Circular needle U.S. size 4. (Metric sizes: 3.5, 4.0, and 3.5 circular.)

GAUGE
U.S. size 6 needles in striped St st: 4" (10 cm.) = 19 sts x 25 rows.
To save time, take time to check gauge!

BODY
(Worked from sleeve end to sleeve end):
Beg at left sleeve. With smaller size needles and MC, cast on 44 sts and work 1-1/2" in 1/1 ribbing, inc 24 sts evenly spaced across last wrong side of work row. You now have 68 sts.
Change to larger size needles, work in striped St st as foll: 11 rows in MC, *14 rows in A, 14 rows in MC*, rep * to * throughout. **At the same time**, inc 1 st at each edge of every 5th row, 5 (8, 10) times. Inc 1 st at each edge of every 4th row 9 (6, 4) times. At each edge of every 2nd row, cast on 2 sts 3 times, cast on 3 sts once, cast on 4 sts once,

cast on 5 sts once, cast on 29 sts once = 190 sts. Piece will measure 13-1/4" (13-3/4", 14") from beg. Work even.
Shape Neck: When piece measures 18-1/2"(18-3/4", 19-1/4") from beg, bind off center 2 sts. Join 2nd ball of yarn to 2nd part and work at the same time. At each neck edge of every 2nd row, dec 1 st 3 times. At each neck edge of every 4th row, dec 1 st twice. At each neck edge of every 5th row, dec 1 st twice = 87 sts. Work even until piece measures 24-1/2" (25-1/4", 26") from beg, mark edge as center of work. Work 2nd half to correspond, increasing at neck edge instead of decreasing = 94 sts on each half. Rejoin halves casting on 2 sts between them = 190 sts. Work until piece measures 22" (22-3/4", 23-1/2") from side seam. Bind off 29 sts at beg of next 2 rows, bind off 5 sts at beg of next 2 rows, bind off 4 sts at beg of next 2 rows, bind off 3 sts at beg of next 2 rows, bind off 2 sts at beg of next 6 rows. Dec 1 st at each edge of every 4th row 9 (6, 4) times. Dec 1 st at each edge of every 5th row 5 (8, 10) times = 68 sts. Work even until piece measures 11-3/4"(12-1/4", 12-1/2") from side seam. Change to smaller size needles and MC and work 1-1/2" in 1/1 ribbing, dec 24 sts evenly spaced across first row = 44 sts. Bind off loosely.

FINISHING
Embroider in duplicate st foll charts. Chart 1 shows

vertical flowers and chart 2 shows horizontal flowers. For chart 1, work from right to left. For chart 2, work from lower edge to upper edge. Place flowers wherever you desire, using the photo as a guide.
Lower Ribbing: With smaller size needles and MC, pick up and knit 86 sts along lower edge of back. Work 2-1/2" in 1/1 ribbing, bind off loosely. Work same ribbing along lower edge of front. With circular needle and MC, pick up and knit 124 (130, 136) sts around neck and work 1" in 1/1 ribbing. Bind off loosely.
Sew side and sleeve seams.

KEY TO CHARTS
G = MC
Z = A
L = B
O = C
X = D
□ = E

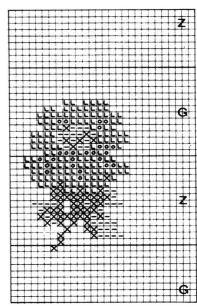

CHART 2

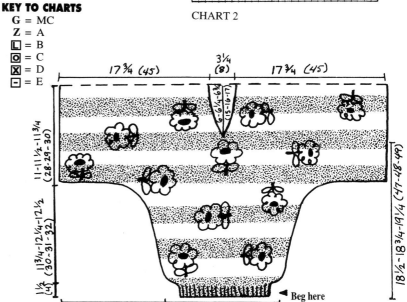

RELAXING

Autumn

Country wildflowers blend

beautifully with the cable

border of this cardigan.

SIZES
■ Small (Medium, Large)
■ Finished bust measurements: 45-1/2" (51", 56-1/2")
■ Finished length: 28-1/4" (28-1/4", 29")
■ Finished sleeve length: 17-3/4"

MATERIALS
■ Scheepjeswol Voluma (50 g): 11 (12, 12) balls Graygreen (double strand) - MC
■ Anchor tapestry wool skeins: salmon-9, red-13, light rose-23, light rosewood-28, lilac-96, light purple-105, blue green-186, light blue green-202, soft green-240, green-243, light green-265, light yellow-305, light maize-311, brown-350, light brown-368, soft yellow-386, white-402, light gray-431, purple-575, rose-642, rose red-644, pine green-654, medium green-733, pale pink-740, light orange-746, gray green-837, dark gray green-862, golden brown-3001, rust brown-3025, yellow green-3097, light lilac-3154, moss green-3236.
■ U.S. size 8 and 10 knitting needles. 36" Circular needle U.S. size 8 and 10, double-pointed needles U.S. needle 8 and 10. (Metric sizes: 5.0, 6.0, and 5.0 and 6.0 90 cm. circular and double-pointed needles.) Cable needle. Stitch holder.
■ 7 buttons.
■ Knit fabric 2-3/4" x 32".

GAUGE
U.S. size 10 needles in St st: 4" (10 cm.) = 14 sts x 19 rows.
To save time, take time to check gauge!

BODY
Work back and forth in 1 piece, using circular needles to accomodate all sts. With smaller size circular needle and Voluma (double strand), cast on 165 (179, 193) sts and work as foll, wrong side facing: 1 border st, p6, *k4, p3*, rep * to * 20 (22, 24) times, end with k4, p6, 1 border st. Continue by working in cable stitch by foll chart 1 as foll: 1 border st, 6 sts in St st, then work point 2 to point 5, 10 (11, 12) times, work from point 2 to 3 once, 6 sts in St st, 1 border st. When border measures 1-1/4", make the first buttonhole. With right side facing, work 3 sts, bind off 2 sts. Work to end of row. On foll row, cast on 2 sts over bound off sts. Inc 6 (12, 18) sts evenly spaced across last wrong side of work row = 171 (191, 211) sts.
Change to larger size circular needle, work chart 2 as foll: 1 border st, 6 sts in St st 157 (177, 197) sts foll chart 2 [work between point 1 to point 2 (3, 4) once, between point 5 (6, 7) and 2 (3, 4) once, and

between point 5 (6, 7) to 8 once], 6 sts in St st, 1 border st. Omit flower motifs. At the same time, at right edge of right side rows, make 5 buttonholes same as the first, spaced 4-1/4" apart.
Shape Armholes: When piece measures 17" (16-1/2", 17") from beg-point B (A, B) on chart, work across first 44 (49, 54) sts for right front, place these sts on holder. Bind off 2 sts, work across next 79 (89, 99) sts for back, place these sts on holder. Bind off 2 sts, work across rem 44 (49, 54) sts for left front. At right edge of every 2nd row, dec 1 st twice = 42 (47, 52) sts.
Shape Neck: When left front measures 26" (26", 26-3/4") from beg-point C (C, D) on chart, with wrong side facing, place first 7 sts on holder. At neck edge of every 2nd row, bind off 5 (6, 7) sts once, bind off 2 sts 3 times, dec 1 st once.
Shape Shoulder: When left front measures 27-1/2" (27-1/2", 28-1/4") from beg-point E (E, F), bind off 12 (14, 16) sts once, bind off 11 (13, 15) sts once. Pick up sts on holder for right front and work to correspond, rev shapings and omitting buttonholes. Pick

up sts on holder for back. At each edge of every 2nd row, dec 1 st twice = 75 (85, 95) sts. Work even. When piece measures 10-1/2" (11", 11-1/4") from beg of armhole, end wrong side of work.
Shape Neck: Bind off center 23 (25, 27) sts. Join 2nd ball of yarn to 2nd part and work at the same time. At each neck edge of every 2nd row, bind off 3 sts once. At the same time, Shape Shoulders: At armhole edge of every 2nd row, bind off 12 (14, 16) sts once, bind off 11 (13, 15) sts once.

SLEEVE
With smaller size double pointed needles and MC, cast on 39 sts, mark beg of round. Work first round as foll: *k1, p4, k3, p4, k1*, work * to * 3 times total. Continue by foll chart 1: work from point 1 to 4, 3 times.
Change to larger size double pointed needles, work by foll chart 2: work from point 9 to 10, beg at point G. Inc 1 st each edge of every marked st on every 2nd round 0 (4, 6) times. Inc 1 st each edge of marked st every 4th round 17 (15, 14) times. Work new sts in St st as you inc = 73 (77, 79) sts.

When sleeve measures 17-3/4" from beg, work back and forth.
Shape Sleeve Top: Bind off 6 sts at beg of next 8 rows. Bind off rem 25 (29, 31) sts.

FINISHING
Embroider pieces by foll chart 2, using the following directions as a guide. A = the branches in chain st and stems in stem stitch in moss green, the shadows in salmon in outline st and the flowers in duplicate st.

KEY TO CHART:
Charts show all rows
□ k1 on right side, p1 on wrong side
⊟ p1 on right side, k1 on wrong side

☑ Cross 2 Right: Knit the 2nd st by passing RH needle in front of the first st, purl the first st
◺ Cross 2 left: Sl 1 st onto cable needle and hold at front of work, p1, k1 from cable needle
◩ light rose - 23
◪ light rosewood - 28
▨ lilac - 96
▧ light purple - 105
⊡ soft green-240
⊠ light green-265
⊡ light yellow-305
⊡ light maize-311
⊡ light brown-368
⊡ soft yellow-386,
⊡ white -402
⊡ pale pink-740
⊙ gray green-837
⊡ yellow green-3097
⊞ light lilac-3154
⊠ salmon-9

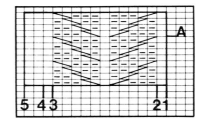

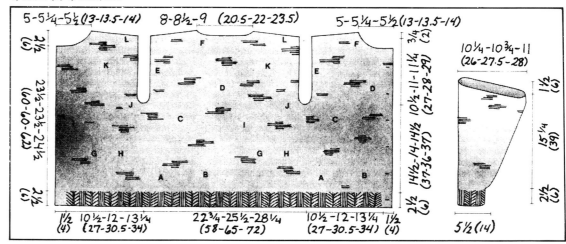

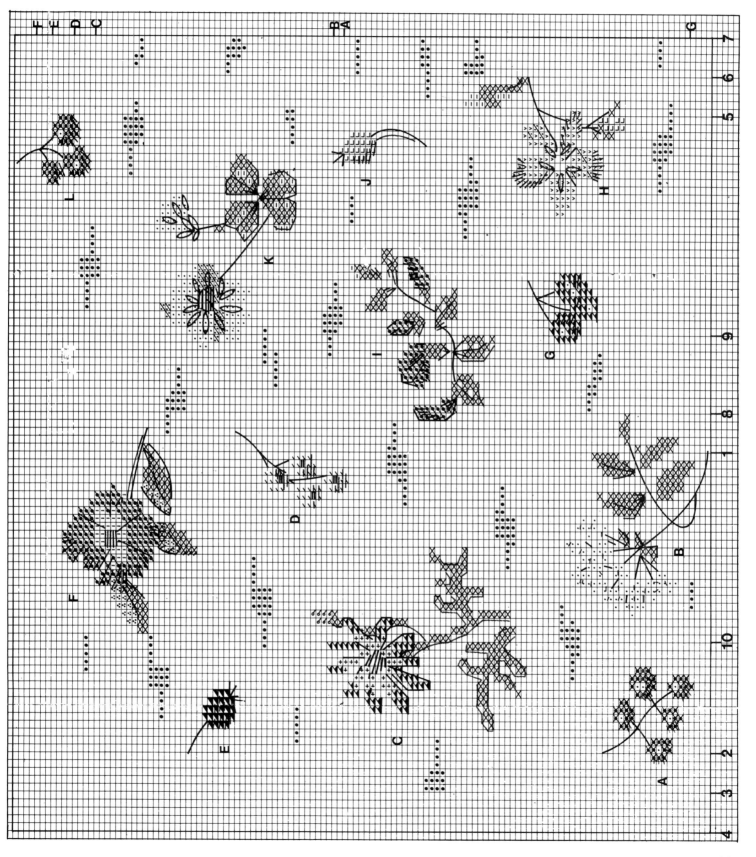

B = the stem under the white flower in chain st and the veins in the white flower in outline st with blue green, the yellow center in small outline st in light maize, the center of the leaves in chain st in golden brown and the veins in the leaves in stem st in moss green. C = the outline of the stem in green, moss green and light green. Along the underside of the petals and scattered in the flowers work in stem st in purple, the centers in satin stitch in light yellow. D = The stems in stem st in brown, the shadows in satin stitch in golden brown and brown. E = the stem in chain st in light blue green, the center of stem in outline st in yellow green and the flower in satin stitch in red, pale pink and yellow green. F = the stem in chain st in green, along the stem and the leaves a line in stem stitch in soft green, the veins in the leaves in stem st and the shadows in the petals in stem st and satin st in pink and the centers in stem st in light green. G = the stems in chain st in green and the shadows in satin st in purple. H = the sprigs in chain stitch and the veins in the leaves in stem st in medium green and the petals in chain st in medium green and light brown the petal shadows in satin st in light brown. I = the sprigs in chain st in brown the veins in the petals in stem st and outline st in blue green and light blue green, the shadows of the petals in outline st and satin st in pink and rose red. J = the sprigs in chain st in light green, a line in stem st in gray green, the shadow in outline st in light orange and the crowns in outline st in rust brown. K = the stems in chain st in golden brown, the center of the big flower in satin st in light yellow and outline st in medium green. Around the center in chain st in light gray, under the small white flower in chain st in soft green and blue green and the flower in chain st in light gray, around the petals in stem st with

medium green and the vein in stem st in outline st in moss green. L = the sprigs in chain st with light green and the shadows in outline st in rose red. On the sleeves, work the lower left flower F, right center flower K, left upper flower I and upper center flower G foll chart 2.
Sew shoulder seams. With smaller size circular needle, pick up and knit 90 (95, 95) sts around neck, including sts from holders. Work as foll: 1 border st, 6 sts in St st, 76 (81, 81) sts in cable st by foll chart 1: work from point 2 to point 4 (5, 5) 1 (5, 5) times, point 1 (2, 2) to point 3 once, 0 (6, 6) sts in St st, 1 border st. Work for 1-1/4", then make a buttonhole above previous ones. Work to point A of chart. Bind off loosely. Sew knit fabric to inside of front bands, folding under 1/4" along all edges covering 6 sts. Whip stitch to fronts with gray green tapestry wool. Cut openings for buttonholes and whip stitch edges, making 3 satin stitches at each end of buttonholes. Sew in sleeves. Sew on buttons.

EFFERVESCENT

Fun flowers in a lattice pattern are simple to embroider on a purchased pullover.

MATERIALS
■ Purchased pullover
■ DMC embroidery floss: 1 skein each light pink-7102, yellow-7470, purple-7896, green-7952.
■ Tracing paper, ruler, triangle, basting thread

Measure the width and length of the pullover and transfer the measurements to tracing paper. Draw a line down the center. Draw 2 diagonal lines each at a forty-five degree angle to center line beginning at center neck. Mark dots 4" apart along each diagonal line. Join the dots to form diamonds over entire front. Pin the tracing paper to the front. With basting thread, mark the diagonal lines. Remove the paper. Alternately embroider large pink and yellow flowers in daisy stitch at all intersections. Between the intersections, embroider smaller flowers and leaves with stem stitch joining flowers. Use the photo as a guide for color selection and placement of flowers.

yellow

purple

green

light pink

motifs

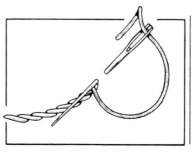

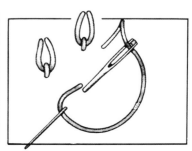

50

COUNTRY

⚘ COUNTRY

The always-popular combination of dark blue and white create the natural symplicity of this floral sweater.

SIZES
■ Small (Medium, Large)
■ Finished bust measurements: 41-1/2" (45", 48")
■ Finished length: 26 - 3/4"
■ Finished sleeve length: 17-3/4"

MATERIALS
■ Mayflower Felina (50 g): 12 (13, 14) balls Blue - MC; 1 ball Ecru - CC
■ U.S. size 4 and 6 knitting needles. 16" Circular needle U.S. size 3 and 4. (Metric sizes: 3.5, 4.0, and 3.0 and 3.5 40 cm. circular.)

GAUGE
U.S. size 6 needles in St st: 4" (10 cm.) = 20 sts x 28 rows.
To save time, take time to check gauge!

BACK
With smaller size needles and MC, cast on 96 (100, 104) sts and work 2-3/4" in 1/1 ribbing. Purl 1 row on wrong side of work, inc 12 (16, 20) sts evenly spaced across row = 108 (116, 124) sts.
Change to larger size needles, work in St st.
Shape Armholes: When back measures 16" (15-3/4", 15-1/4") from beg, bind off 3 sts at beg of next 2 rows. Bind off 2 sts at beg of next 2 rows. Dec 1 st at each edge of every 2nd row twice = 94 (102, 110) sts.
Shape Shoulders: When back measures 9-1/4" (9-3/4", 10-1/4") from beg of armhole, bind off 6 (7, 8) sts at beg of next 2 (4, 6) rows, bind off 7 (8, 9) sts at beg of next 6 (4, 2) rows. **At the same time,** when back measures 26-1/2" from beg, bind off center 38 (40, 42) sts. At each neck edge of every 2nd row, dec 1 st once.

FRONT
Beg front same as back, but beg chart above ribbing as foll: work 1 border st, then work from point 1 (2, 3) to point 4 (5, 6), end with 1 border st. Beg at point A (B, C). When piece measures 16" (15-3/4", 15-1/4") - point D on chart, carry unused yarn loosely across back of work. **At the same time,** shape armholes as on back.
Shape Neck: When front measures 9" (9-1/4", 9-3/4") from beg of armhole, bind off center 28 (30, 32) sts. Join 2nd ball of yarn to 2nd part and work at the same time. At each neck edge of every 2nd row, bind off 3 sts once, bind off 2 sts once, dec 1 st once. **At the same time,** Shape shoulders as on back.

SLEEVES
With smaller size needles and MC, cast on 48 sts, work 2" in 1/1 ribbing. Purl 1 row on wrong side of work, inc 8 (10, 12) sts evenly spaced across row = 56 (58, 60) sts.
Change to larger size needles, work in St st. Inc 1 st each edge of every 6th row 16 (14, 12) times. Inc 1 st at each edge of every 4th row 3 (6, 9) times. Work new sts in St st as you inc = 94 (98, 102) sts.
When sleeve measures 17-3/4" from beg, end wrong side of work row.
Shape Sleeve Top: Bind off 3 sts at beg of next 2 rows. Bind off 4 sts at beg of next 4 rows. Bind off 5 sts at beg of next 8 rows. Bind off 6 (7, 8) sts at beg of next 2 rows. Bind off rem 20 (22, 24) sts.

FINISHING
Sew shoulder seams.
Neckband: With smaller size circular needle and MC, pick up and knit 112 (116, 120) sts around neck. Work 1-1/4" in rev St st, then change to larger size circular needle and work until neckband measures 2-3/4", then bind off loosely. Fold in half to outside and blind stitch in place. Set in sleeves, matching center of sleeve to shoulder seam. Sew side and sleeve seams.

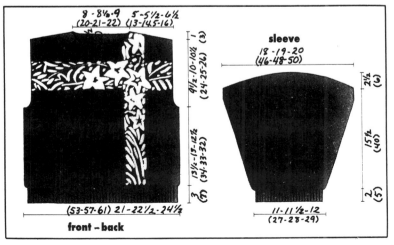

KEY TO CHART
- ☐ MC
- ☒ CC

❁ IRRESISTIBLE

The colors of the Orient

make a striking background

for a rose motif.

SIZES
■ 5 (6, 7) years
■ Finished chest measurements: 27-1/2" (29-1/2", 31-1/2")
■ Finished length: 17" (18-3/4", 21")
■ Finished sleeve length: 11-1/2" (12-1/2", 13-3/4")

MATERIALS
■ Scheepjeswol Superwash Zermatt (50 g): 4(5,5) balls Red - MC; 1 ball each Rose - A, Ecru - B, Blue Green - C, Blue - D and Dark Blue - E
■ Anchor Tapestry Wool salmon - 09, bright rose - 023, rose - 063, dark rose - 064, green - 0243, light green - 0265, light pink - 0642, and dark green - 3388
■ U.S. size 3 and 5 knitting needles. 16" Circular needle U.S. size 3. (Metric sizes: 3.0, 3.75, and 3.0 40 cm. circular.)

GAUGE
U.S. size 5 needles in St st: 4" (10 cm.) = 20 sts x 29 rows.
To save time, take time to check gauge!

BACK
With smaller size needles and MC, cast on 62 (64, 66) sts and work 2" (2-1/2", 2-1/2") in 1/1 ribbing. Purl 1 row across wrong side of work, inc 10 (13, 16) sts evenly spaced across row = 72 (77, 82) sts.
Change to larger size needles, work in striped St st as foll: 0 (2, 6) rows in MC, 8 rows foll chart 1, beg with 1 border st, then point 1 (2, 3) to point 4, 1 border st. [For size 5 and 7 dec 1 (inc 1) on last row of chart.] Work 4 rows foll chart 2 as foll: 1 border st, point 1 to point 7, 23 (25, 27) times, 1 border st. Work 1 row in B. [For size 5 and 7, inc 1 (dec 1) st.] Work 70 (76, 80) rows in MC. Work 7 rows foll chart 4 as foll: 1 border st, then point 1 (2, 3) to point 4 (5, 6), 1 border st. Work 2 rows in MC. (For size 6, inc 1 st.) Work 2 rows foll chart 5 as foll: 1 border st, work from point 1 to point 2, 17 (19, 20) times, 1 border st. (For size 5, work from point 1 to point 3 once.) Work 16 (20, 26) rows in MC, dec in the first row in MC 0 (0, 1) sts = 110 (122, 136) rows. Carry unused yarns loosely across wrong side of work.
When back measures 17" (18-3/4", 20-3/4") from beg, bind off all sts.

FRONT
Beg front same as back, but work the 8 rows foll chart 1 for size 7 as foll: 1 border st, then rep points 3 to 5, 1 border st.
Shape Neck: When front measures 15" (17", 18-3/4") from beg, bind off center 16 (19, 22) sts. Join 2nd ball of yarn to 2nd part and work at the same time. At each neck edge of every 2nd row, bind off 3 sts at beg of next 2 rows, bind off 2 sts at beg of next 2 rows, dec 1 st twice.
Shape Shoulders: When front measures 17" (18-3/4", 20-3/4") from beg, bind off rem 21 (22, 23) sts on each shoulder.

SLEEVE
With smaller size needles and MC, cast on 40 (42, 44) sts, work 1-1/2" (2", 2") in 1/1 ribbing. Purl 1 row on wrong side of work, inc 10 sts evenly spaced across row = 50 (52, 54) sts.
Change to larger size needles, work in striped St st centering all charts at point 7 as foll: 6 (7, 8) rows in E; 8 rows foll chart 1; 4 rows foll chart 2; 1 row in B; 27 (29, 32) rows in MC; 7 rows foll the left half of chart 2; 7 rows foll the right half of chart 2; 2 rows in MC; 2 rows foll chart 5; complete in MC. At the same time, inc 1 st each edge of every 6th row 7 (8, 8) times. Inc 1 st each edge of every 8th row 3 (3, 4) times. Work new sts in St st as you inc = 70 (74, 78) sts.
When sleeve measures 11-1/2" (12-1/2", 13-3/4") from beg, bind off all sts.

FINISHING
Embroider back foll chart 3. Beg embroidery on the 23rd (29th, 35th) row above ribbing. Embroider rose motif on front foll chart 6. Beg embroidery on the 16th (21st, 27th) row above ribbing, centering chart at point M1 (M, M1). Sew shoulder seams. With circular needle and MC, pick up and knit 80 (86, 92) sts around neck. Work 3-1/4" in 1/1 ribbing, bind off. Fold neckband in half to inside and slip stitch in place. Sew sleeves to side seams, matching center of sleeve to shoulder seam. Sew side and sleeve seams.

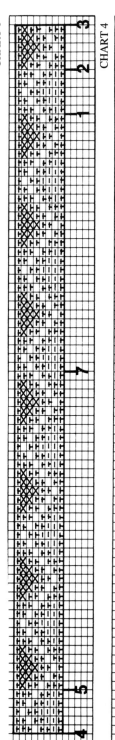

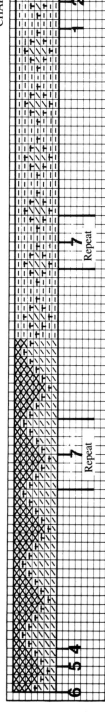

6-6½-7 (15-16.5-18)

13¾-14-15 (34-36-38)

15-16¼-18¼ (38-42-47)

2-2½-2½ (5-6-6)

10-10½-11¾ (25-27-30)

1½-2-2 (4-5-5)

13¾-14¾-15¾ (35-37.5-40)

9¼-9¾-10¼ (24-25-26)

56

CHART 3

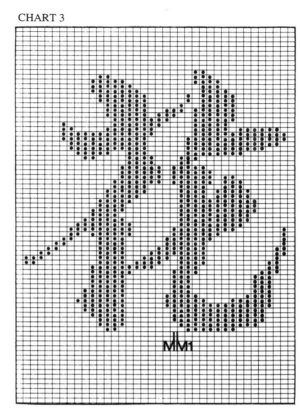

MM1

CHART 5

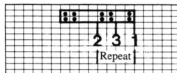

2 3 1
|Repeat|

CHART 2

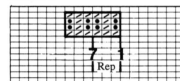

7 1
|Rep|

CHART 6

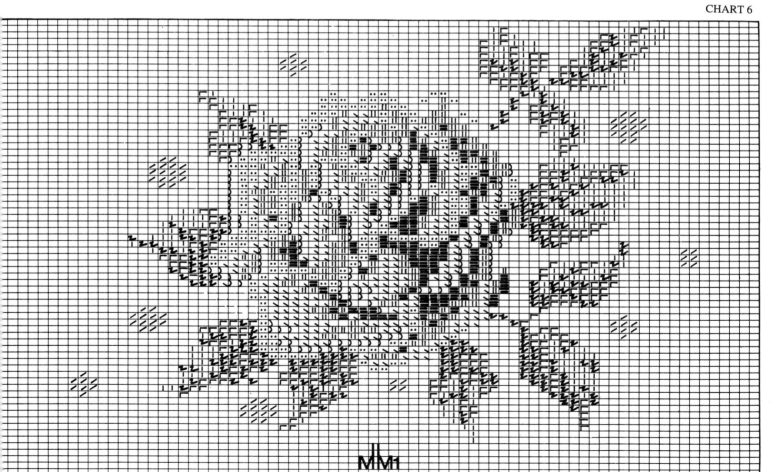

MM1

SPIRITED

Small motifs and pattern bands are set off by an array of large, wild asters.

SIZES
- Small (Medium, Large, Extra Large)
- Finished bust measurements: 41" (44", 47", 50-1/2")
- Finished length: 26-1/2"
- Finished sleeve length: 18-1/2"

MATERIALS
- Scheepjeswol Invicta Extra (50 g): 8 (8, 9, 9) balls Dark Blue - MC; 3 balls Ecru - CC
- Tapestry wool in desired colors for flower motif
- U.S. size 2 and 3 knitting needles. Circular needle U.S. size 2. (Metric sizes: 2.5, 3.0, and 2.5 circular.)

GAUGE
U.S. size 3 needles in Fairisle St st: 4" (10 cm.) = 28 sts x 36 rows.
To save time, take time to check gauge!

BACK
With smaller size needles and MC, cast on 158 (170, 182, 194) sts and work 1-1/2" in St st. Purl 1 row across right side of work, then work 3 rows in St st in MC. Continue by foll chart 2: 1 border st, work point 1 to point 2, 6 (7, 7, 8) times, then work point 1 to point 3, 1 (0, 1, 0) times, 1 border st. Carry unused yarn loosely across wrong side of work. When chart is complete, work 2 rows in MC, then work chart 2 once, work 2 rows in MC. Change to larger size needles, work in fairisle St st foll chart 1, beg with 1 border st, work point 1 to point 2, 19 (21, 22, 24) times, then work point 1 to 3, 1 (0, 1, 0) time, end with 1 border st.

When back measures 28" from beg, bind off all sts.

FRONT
Beg front same as back, but work chart 2 as foll: 1 border st, point 3 to point 2, 1 (0, 1, 0) time, point 1 to point 2, 6 (7, 7, 8) times, 1 border st. Then work chart 1 as foll: 1 border st, point 3 to point 2, 1 (0, 1, 0) time, point 1 to point 2, 19 (21, 22, 24) times, 1 border st. Shape armholes as on back.

Shape Neck: When front measures 26-1/2" from beg, bind off center 38 (40, 42, 44) sts. Join 2nd ball of yarn to 2nd part and work at the same time. At each neck edge of every 2nd row, bind off 6 sts once, bind off 4 sts once, bind off 3 sts once, bind off 2 sts twice.

Shape Shoulders: When front measures 28" from beg, bind off rem 43 (48, 53, 58) sts on each shoulder.

SLEEVE
With smaller size needles and MC, cast on 71 (74, 77, 80) sts, work 1-1/2" in St st, then purl 1 row on right side of work, then work 3 rows in MC in St st. Center chart 2 at point 4 (3, 4, 3). Work chart 2 once, work 2 rows in MC, work chart 2 once, work 1 row in MC. Purl the foll wrong side of work row in MC, inc 7 (8, 9, 10) sts evenly spaced across row = 78 (82, 86, 90) sts. Change to larger size needles, work in striped St st as foll: *work 40 rows of chart 1, work 2 rows of MC, work 5 rows of chart 2, 2 rows of MC*, rep * to *, end with 5 rows of chart 2. **At the same time,** inc 1 st each edge of every 4th row 20 (19, 18,17) times. Inc 1 st each edge of every 2nd row 22 (24, 26, 28) times. Work new sts in striped St st as you inc = 162 (168, 174, 180) sts. When sleeve measures 21-1/2" from beg, bind off all sts.

FINISHING
Trace flower motif on tissue paper. Pin to upper right side of front. Run a basting thread around outlines of flowers and leaves. Remove tissue paper and embroider flowers and leaves in satin stitch. Use photo as a guide. Sew shoulder seams. With circular needle and MC, pick up and knit 162 (168, 174, 180) sts around neck. Work 2 rounds in St st in MC, work chart 2 once, work 2 rounds of St st in MC, purl 1 round in MC, then work 20 rounds of MC from beg. Bind off loosely. Fold neckband in half to inside and slip stitch in place. Sew sleeves to side seams, matching center of sleeve to shoulder seam. Sew side and sleeve seams. Fold lower borders to inside and slip stitch in place.

Chart 1

2 3 1

repeat

KEY TO CHARTS
- ☐ MC
- ⊡ CC

Chart 2

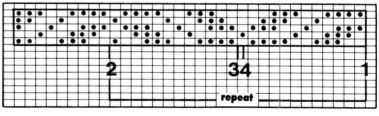

2 34 1

repeat

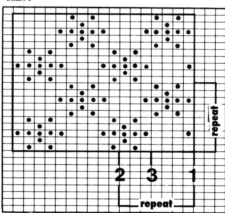

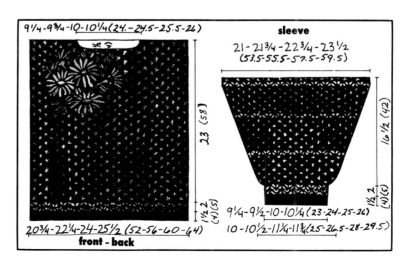

9¼-9¾-10-10¼ (24.-24.5-25.5-26)

sleeve
21-21¾-22¾-23½ (53.5-55.5-57.5-59.5)

23 (58)

16½ (42)

1½ (4)

9¼-9½-10-10¼ (23-24-25-26)
10-10½-11¼-11¾ (25-26.5-28-29.5)

20¾-22¼-24-25½ (52-56-60-64)
front - back

1½ (4)

TAPESTRY

An old-fashioned style rose embroidered in duplicate stitch adds a tapestry look to this pullover.

SIZES
- Small/Medium (Large)
- Finished bust measurements: 45-1/2" (48")
- Finished length: 24-3/4"
- Finished sleeve length: 17-1/4"

MATERIALS
- Mayflower Cotton 8 (50 g): 10 (11) balls Gray—MC
- Angora (20 g, 95 yds): 4 balls White - CC
- DMC Embroidery floss: ecru, light orange brown-2436, beige-2642, rust brown-2237, orange brown-2921, light brown-2922, light rose-2574, rose-2572, dark rose-2570, dark red-2497, gray rose-2373, red brown-2221, gray green-2928, dark gray green-2926, bright dark brown-2371, dark brown-2898, dark blue green-2500, light yellow-2446, yellow-2726, light green-2472, green-2470, dark ecru-2613, purple-2531, lilac-2231, gray purple-2398, dark olive green-2511, olive green-2392, dark green-2890, white.
- U.S. size 2 and 3 knitting needles. 16" Circular needle U.S. size 2. (Metric sizes: 2.5, 3.0, and 2.5 40 cm. circular.)

GAUGE
U.S. size 3 needles in fairisle St st: 4" (10 cm.) = 25 sts x 32 rows.
To save time, time time to check gauge!

BACK
With smaller size needles and MC, cast on 126 (132) sts and work 2" in 1/1 ribbing, inc 20 (22) sts evenly spaced across last wrong side of work row = 146 (154) sts.
Change to larger size needles, work in fairisle St st foll chart, beg and end with 1 border st. Beg right side of work rows with point A, beg wrong side of work rows with point B. Work repeat across. Carry yarn not in use loosely across wrong side of work.
Shape Armholes: When back measures 15-3/4" (15-1/4") from beg, bind off 3 (4) sts at beg of next 2 rows. Bind off 2 sts at beg of next 4 (6) rows. Dec 1 st at each edge of every 2nd row, 3 (2) times = 126 (130) sts.
Shape Neck: When back measures 9" (9-1/4") from beg of armhole, end with 1 row of MC, bind off all sts, marking center 46 (48) sts for neck.

FRONT
Beg front same as back. The flower motif will be embroidered later beg 6" from lower edge. Work entirely in MC over the area which will be embroidered later. If necessary, the small motifs can be duplicate stitched around edges of motif.
Shape Neck: When front measures 6-1/2" (7") from beg of armhole, bind off center 30 (32) sts. Join 2nd ball of yarn to 2nd part and work at the same time. At each neck edge of every 2nd row bind off 3 sts once, bind off 2 sts once, dec 1 st 3 times.
Shape Shoulders: When front measures 9" (9-1/4") from beg of armhole, end with 1 row of MC, bind off 40 (41) sts on each shoulder.

SLEEVE
With smaller size needles and MC, cast on 52 (56) sts, work 2" in 1/1 ribbing, inc 25 sts evenly spaced across last wrong side of work row = 77 (81) sts.
Change to larger size needles, work in fairisle St st centering chart. Inc 1 st each edge of every 3/4" 20 (21) times. Work new sts in fairisle St st as you inc = 117 (123) sts. End with 2 rows of St st in MC.
When sleeve measures 17-1/4" from beg, end wrong side of work row.
Shape Sleeve Top: Bind off 3 (4) sts at beg of next 2 rows. Bind off 2 sts at beg of next 4 rows. Dec 1 st at each edge of every 2nd row 4 times. End with 2 rows of St st in MC. Bind off rem 95 (99) sts.

FINISHING
Embroider front in duplicate st centering chart. Beg 6" from lower edge. Sew shoulder seams.
Neckband: With circular needle and MC, pick up and knit 132 (136) sts around neck. Work 2-1/2" in 1/1 ribbing, bind off. Fold neckband in half to inside and slip st in place. Set in sleeves, matching center of sleeve to shoulder seam. Sew side and sleeve seams.

KEY TO CHART
- ▫ ecru
- light orangebrown-2436
- ☑ beige-2642
- rust brown-2237
- ☑ orange brown-2921
- ◪ light brown-2922
- ☐ light rose-2574
- ☒ rose-2572
- ☒ dark rose-2570
- ▣ dark red-2497
- ☐ gray rose-2373
- ☑ red brown-2221
- ☑ gray green-2928
- ☒ dark gray green-2926
- ◤ bright dark brown-2371
- ◪ dark brown-2898
- ☐ dark blue green-2500
- ☐ light yellow-2446
- ☒ yellow-2726
- ◩ light green-2472
- ☑ green-2470
- ☐ dark ecru-2613
- ☐ purple-2531
- ☒ lilac-2231
- ◤ gray purple-2398
- ◪ dark olive green-2511
- ☒ olive green-2392
- ▦ dark green-2890
- ▫ white

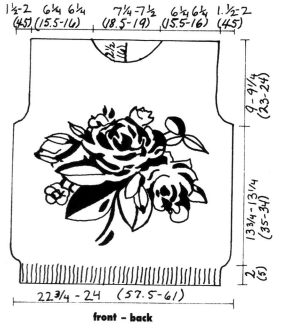

1½-2 (4-5) · 6¼ 6¼ (15.5-16) · 7¼-7½ (18.5-19) · 6¼ 6¼ (15.5-16) · 1½-2 (4-5)

9-9¼ (23-24)

13¾-13¼ (35-34)

2 (5)

22¾-24 (57.5-61)

front – back

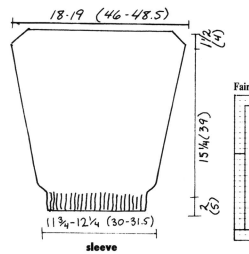

18-19 (46-48.5)

1½ (4)

15¼ (39)

2 (5)

11¾-12¼ (30-31.5)

sleeve

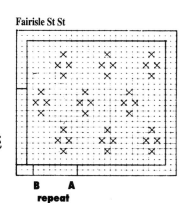

Fairisle St St

B · A
repeat

SIMPLE

SIMPLE

Charming ecru duplicate stitch flowers are set off against a navy blue background.

SIZES
- 4 (6, 7) years
- Finished chest measurements: 29" (30-1/2", 32")
- Finished length: 15" (17", 18-1/2")
- Finished sleeve length: 10-3/4" (12", 13-1/4")

MATERIALS
- Mayflower Felina (50 g): 5 (6, 7) balls Blue - MC; 1 ball Ecru - CC
- U.S. size 4 and 6 knitting needles. 16" Circular needle U.S. size 3. (Metric sizes: 3.5, 4.0, and 3.0 40 cm. circular.)

GAUGE
U.S. size 6 needles in St st: 4" (10 cm.) = 20 sts x 28 rows.
To save time, take time to check gauge!

BACK
With smaller size needles and MC, cast on 62 (66, 70) sts and work 1-1/4" (1-1/2", 2") in 1/1 ribbing, inc 14 sts evenly spaced across last wrong side of work row. You now have 76 (80, 84) sts.
Change to larger size needles, work in St st.
Shape Armholes: When back measures 8" (9-3/4", 10-1/2") - 48 (56, 62) rows above border, bind off 2 sts at beg of next 2 rows. Dec 1 st at each edge of every 2nd row 2 (3, 4) times. You now have 68 (70, 72) sts.
Shape Shoulders: When back measures 6-1/4" (6-1/2", 7") from beg of armhole, bind off 6 sts at beg of next 4 rows. Bind off 7 sts at beg of next 2 rows. Bind off rem 30 (32, 34) sts for neck.

FRONT
Beg front same as back. Shape armholes as on back. Work 40 (42, 42) rows from beg of armhole, end wrong side of work row.
Shape Neck: Bind off center 10 (12, 14) sts. Join 2nd ball of yarn to 2nd part and work at the same time. At each neck edge of every 2nd row, bind off 4 sts once, bind off 3 sts once, bind off 2 sts once, dec 1 st once.
Shape shoulders as on back.

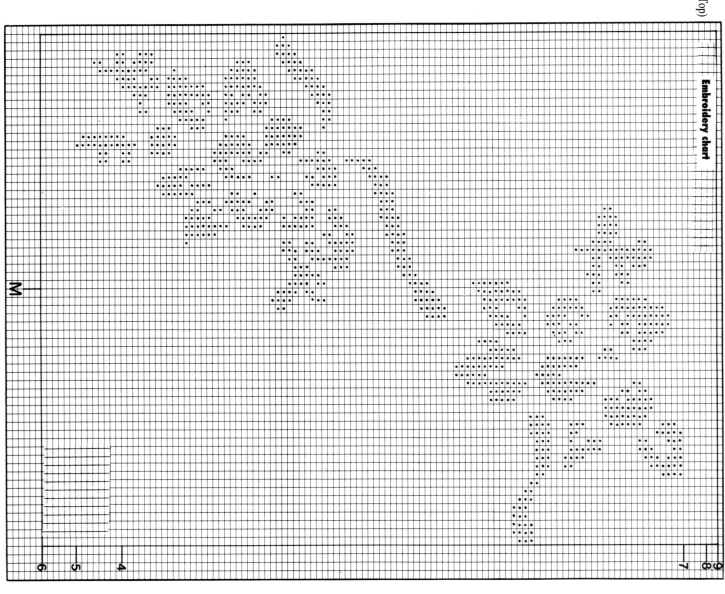

Embroidery chart

(Top)

SLEEVE

With smaller size needles and MC, cast on 32 (34, 36) sts, work 1-1/4" (1-1/2", 2") in 1/1 ribbing. Purl 1 row on wrong side of work, inc 12 sts evenly spaced across row = 44 (46, 48) sts.

Change to larger size needles, work in St st. Inc 1 st each edge of every 6th row 11 (12, 13) times. Work new sts in St st as you inc = 66 (70, 74) sts.

Shape Sleeve Top: When sleeve measures 10-3/4" (12", 13-1/4") from beg, bind off 3 sts at beg of next 2 (4, 4) rows. Bind off 4 sts at beg of next 2 (2, 4) rows. Bind off 6 (5, 5) sts at beg of next 2 rows. Bind off 9 (9, 7) sts at beg of next 2 rows. Bind off rem 22 sts.

FINISHING

Embroider flower motif in duplicate stitch in CC on front by centering chart at point M. Beg above ribbing at point 4 (5, 6), work to point 7 (8, 9). Sew shoulder seams.

Neckband: With circular needle and MC, pick up and knit 84 (88, 92) sts around neck. Work 2" in rev St st, bind off. Fold neckband to outside and blind stitch in place. Set in sleeves, matching center of sleeve to shoulder seam. Sew side and sleeve seams.

KEY TO CHART

☐ MC

⊡ CC

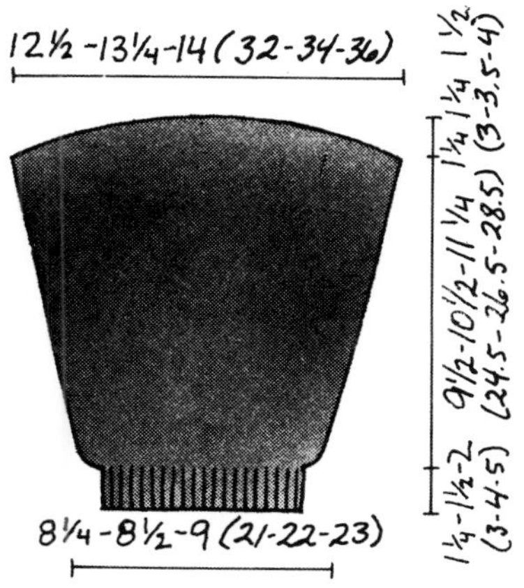
12½-13¼-14 (32-34-36)
1¼ 1¼ 1½ (3-3.5-4)
9½-10½-11¼ (24.5-26.5-28.5)
1¼-1½-2 (3-4-5)
8¼-8½-9 (21-22-23)

sleeve

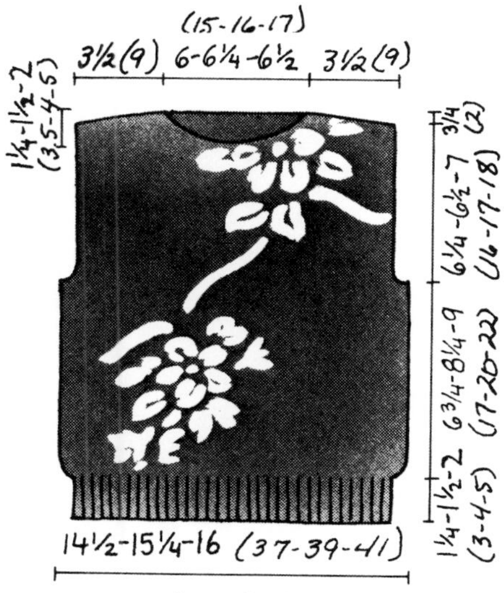
(15-16-17)
3½ (9) 6-6¼-6½ 3½ (9)
1¼-1½-2 (3.5-4-5)
¾ (2)
6¼-6½-7 (16-17-18)
6¾-8¼-9 (17-20-22)
1¼-1½-2 (3-4-5)
14½-15¼-16 (37-39-41)

front - back

DELIGHTFUL

A sprinkling of tiny blooms adorn the front of a purchased cardigan.

MATERIALS

■ Purchased black wool cardigan.

■ DMC embroidery floss: 1 skein each green-368 and light green-369; 2 skeins each light gray-415, pink-776, old rose-778

■ Tracing paper, ruler, triangle, basting thread.

Trace the shape of the fronts of the cardigan on tracing paper. Sketch the positions of flowers on the tracing paper, using the photo as a guide. Pin the tracing paper against outside of the fronts. With basting thread, mark the positions of the flowers. Remove the paper. With embroidery thread, embroider the flower centers in gray, pink or old rose in bullion stitch (long French knots), the stems in stem stitch and the leaves in satin stitch in shades of green. Use the photo as a guide for color selection and placement of flowers.

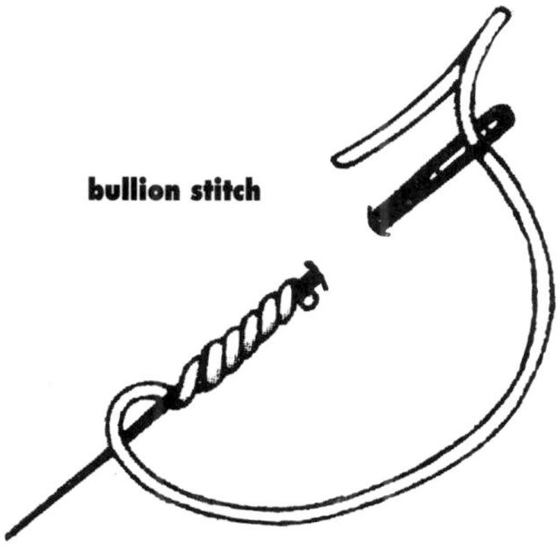

bullion stitch

flower motif

DELIGHTFUL

VINTAGE

Classic rose motifs

complement the nostalgic

shape of this woman's vest.

SIZE
- Medium
- Finished bust measurements: 42"
- Finished back length: 19-3/4"

MATERIALS
- Rowan Double Knitting (50 g): 3 balls Ecru-2 - MC; 2 balls Yellow-6 - A; 1 ball each Lilac-128 - B, Rose Red-66 - C, Gray Green-417 - D, Purple-127 - E, Green-75 - F
- Anchor tapestry wool: 2 skeins dark rose-895, 1 skein rose-629
- U.S. size 2 and 3 knitting needles. Circular needle 36" long U.S. size 2. (Metric sizes: 2.5, 3.0, and 2.5 90 cm. circular.) 4 buttons.

GAUGE
U.S. size 3 needles in St st: 4" (10 cm.) = 27 sts x 36 rows.
To save time, take time to check gauge!

STRIPE PATTERN ON BACK:
1 row B; 2 rows E; 2 rows B; 6 rows MC; 21 rows A; 6 rows MC; 10 rows C; 5 rows foll chart 2; 2 rows E; 31 rows MC; 2 rows MC and C as foll: Row 1: *1 st in MC, 2 sts in C*, rep * to * across. Row 2: work in established color; 5 rows A; 3 rows foll chart 3; 1 row MC; 4 rows D; 6 rows MC; 21 rows A; 6 rows MC; 6 rows C; 7 rows foll chart 1, working from the top down; 3 rows in B; 3 rows in E and B as foll: Row 1: *2 sts in E, 2 sts in B*, rep * to * across. Rows 2 and 3: work in established colors; 18 rows in B = 171 rows.

STRIPE PATTERN ON FRONT:
17 rows in A; 7 rows foll chart 1; 10 rows C; 2 rows in MC; 4 rows in B; then continue in stripe pattern as on back.

BACK
With smaller size needles and MC, cast on 126 sts and work 1" in 1/1 ribbing. Purl 1 row across wrong side of work, inc 20 sts evenly spaced across = 146 sts.
Change to larger size needles, work in stripe pattern as above. When working charts, work 1 border st at each edge. Carry unused yarn loosely across wrong side of work.
Shape Armholes: When back measures 9-1/4"-75 rows above ribbing, bind off 5 sts at beg of next 2 rows, bind off 3 sts at beg of next 2 rows, bind off 2 sts at beg of next 2 rows. Dec 1 st at each edge of every 2nd row 8 times. Dec 1 st at each edge of every 4th row 3 times = 104 sts.
Shape Shoulders: When armhole measures 10" - 167 rows above ribbing, at each armhole edge of every 2nd row, bind off 16 sts once, bind off 17 sts once. On the last row of stripe pattern bind off center 38 sts.

RIGHT FRONT
With larger size needles and A, cast on 3 sts and work in stripe pattern for front. At left edge of every 2nd row, *cast on 2 sts once, cast on 3 sts once*, work * to * 9 times, cast on 2 sts once, cast on 4 sts once. **At the same time,** at right edge of every 2nd row, cast on 1 st once, cast on 2 sts once, cast on 1 st once, cast on 2 sts 6 times, cast on 1 st once = 71 sts.
Shape Neck: When front measures 8-1/2" from beg-78 rows from beg, dec 1 st at neck edge, then *at neck edge of every 6th row, dec 1 st once, at neck edge of every 4th, dec 1 st once*, rep * to * 6 times. At neck edge of every 4th row, dec 1 st once. **At the same time,** when front measures

Chart 1

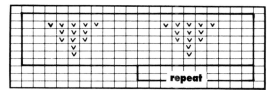
repeat

Chart 2

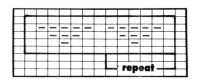
repeat

Chart 3

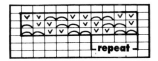
repeat

back
4¾ (12)   5½ (14)   4¾ (12)

¼ (1)
10 (25.5)
10 (25.5)
8¼ (21)
8¼ (21)
4½ (2.5)

21 (53,5)

5 (12)
14½ (37)
center front
6 (16)
2½ (6.5)

10 (25.5)

VINTAGE

8-1/4" measured at left side seam-115 rows at left edge, shape armhole. At left edge of every 2nd row, bind off 5 sts once, bind off 3 sts once, bind off 2 sts once, dec 1 st 8 times. Shape Shoulders: When armhole measures 10"-207 rows from the beg, at armhole edge of every 2nd row, bind off 16 sts once, bind off 17 sts once.

LEFT FRONT
Work same as right front, rev shapings and chart.

FINISHING
Embroider flowers in duplicate stitch foll charts. Beg chart 4 in the 4th row above the first 6 row ecru stripe. Center the charts. For right front, center at MR, for the left front at ML. At the side seams, work leaves instead of half of flower. Beg chart 5 on the 5th row above the 31st row in ecru. Center the chart on left front at ML and right front at MR. Embroider chart 4, but turn it over (see photo) beg on the 8th row above chart 3. Center left front at ML and right front at MR. Sew shoulder seams. With circular needle and MC, pick up and knit 500 sts around neck, center and lower edges of front (about 27 sts every 4"). Work in 1/1 ribbing. Inc 1 st in each cor-

ner on every 2nd round by knitting in the strand between sts at each corner. On the right front, make 4 buttonholes when border measures 1/4" spaced along the straight edge of right front. Place the first buttonhole 1/4" from lower edge and last one at top of straight edge. Space 2 more evenly between top and bottom buttonholes. For each buttonhole, bind off 3 sts. On foll row, cast on 3 sts above bound off sts. When border measures 1", bind off. Sew side seams. With circular needle and MC, pick up and knit 160 sts around armhole and work 1" in 1/1 ribbing. Bind off loosely. Sew on buttons.

KEY TO CHART
- ☐ ecru
- ⊟ green
- ✓ gray green
- ◹ rose red
- ⊠ purple
- ⧄ lilac
- ⧄ dark rose
- ⌊ rose

Chart 4

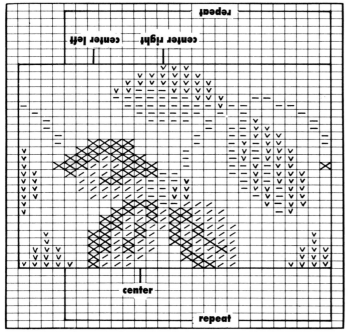

repeat

center left — center right

center

repeat

This Tyrollean jacket with bright embroidered flowers adds color to any day.

SIZES
■ Small (Medium, Large)
■ Finished bust measurements: 43" (45-1/2", 48")
■ Finished length: 24-1/2"
■ Finished sleeve length: 17-3/4"

MATERIALS
■ Scheepjeswol Superwash Zermatt (50 g): 14 (14, 15) balls Red - MC; 1 ball Black -CC
■ Anchor tapestry wool: 1 skein each blue-0133, light green-0239, dark green-0246, yellow-0298, white-0402, pink-0642, light yellow-0656
■ U.S. size 5 knitting needles. Crochet Hook U.S. size D/3. (Metric sizes: 3.75; crochet hook 3.25.) 5 buttons.

GAUGE
U.S. size 5 needles in St st: 4" (10 cm.) = 20 sts x 27 rows.
To save time, take time to check gauge!

BACK
With MC, cast on 112 (118, 124) sts and work in St st.
Shape Armholes: When back measures 14" (13-1/2", 13-1/4") - 96 (93, 90) rows from beg, bind off 3 sts at beg of next 2 rows. Bind off 2 sts at beg of next 2 rows. Dec 1 st at each edge of every 2nd row once = 100 (106, 112) sts.
Shape Shoulders: When back measures 9-1/4" (9-3/4", 10-1/4") from beg of armhole, at each armhole edge of every 2nd row, bind off 15 (16, 17) sts twice. Bind off rem 40 (42, 44) sts for neck.

RIGHT FRONT
With MC, cast on 59 (62, 65) sts and work in St st.

At right edge of right side rows, make 5 buttonholes 3 sts in from right edge. Place the first buttonhole 1-1/4" from lower edge and the last 3/4" from upper edge. Space the others about 5" apart. For each buttonhole, bind off 3 sts. On foll row, cast on 3 sts. **At the same time,** Shape Armhole: When front measures 14" (13-1/2", 13-1/4") - 96 (93, 90) rows from beg, at armhole edge of every 2nd row bind off 3 sts once, bind off 2 sts once, dec 1 st once = 53 (56, 59) sts.
Shape Neck: When front measures 8-1/4" (8-1/2", 9") from beg of armhole, at neck edge of every 2nd row, bind off 13 (14, 15) sts once, bind off 3 sts twice, bind off 2 sts once, dec 1 st twice.
Shape Shoulder: When front measures 9-1/4" (9-3/4", 10-1/4") from beg of armhole, bind off 15 (16, 17) sts twice.

LEFT FRONT
Work same as right front, rev shapings and omitting buttonholes

SLEEVE
With MC, cast on 50 (52, 54) sts, work in St st. Inc 1 st each edge of every 4th row 10 (13, 16) times. Inc 1 st each edge of every 6th row 12 (10, 8) times. Work new sts in St st as you inc = 94 (98, 102) sts.
When sleeve measures 17-3/4", end on wrong side of work row.
Shape Sleeve Top: Bind off 3 sts at beg of next 4 rows. Bind off 4 sts at beg of next 4 rows. Bind off 5 (6, 6) sts at beg of next 2 rows. Bind off 6 (7, 7) sts at beg of next 2 (6, 2) rows. Bind off 7 (0, 8) sts

CLASSIC

at beg of next 4 rows. Bind off rem 16 sts.

FINISHING

Hem stitch around buttonholes in MC. Embroider right front foll chart from point 1 to point 2 (3, 4). Embroider the squares and flower centers in satin stitch: squares in light yellow; yellow flowers with white centers and white flowers with yellow centers. Embroider the petals in daisy st in blue, white or yellow, embroider the stems in chain st foll chart. Embroider the branch with leaves in stem st in light or dark green and the small flowers in satin stitch in pink. For size small, skip the flowers at the left edge and at lower edge. Use the photo as a guide for choice of colors. Embroider the left front to correspond to the right front. Embroider small flowers in white over the 5th to 12th row of sleeves, leaving 4 sts between flowers. Sew shoulder and side seams. With crochet hook and CC, work 3 rows of sc (dc in U.K.) along lower, center front and neck edges. Work 2 sc (dc in U.K.) in each corner and end each round with 1 hdc (dc in U.K.). Beg at 1 side seam.

Fasten off. Set in sleeves and sew sleeve seams. Work same crocheted edge along lower edge. Sew on buttons.

daisy stitch

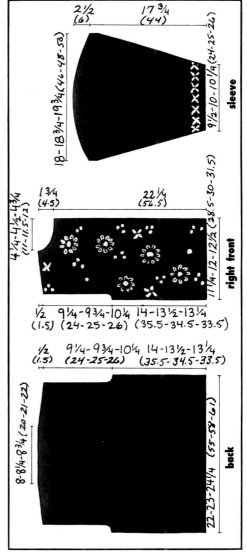

✿✿ TIMELESS

The golden colors in this

floral pullover create a

timeless appeal.

SIZES
■ Small (Medium, Large)
■ Finished bust measurements: 42-1/2" (45-1/2", 49")
■ Finished length: 23-1/2"
■ Finished sleeve length: 17-1/4"

MATERIALS
■ Jaeger Wild Silk (50 g): 10 (10, 11) balls color beige - 2001
■ DMC embroidery floss: 8 skeins each bright blue-955, moss green-3348, light rose-819, light turquoise-747; 5 skeins medium-green-912; 4 skeins each soft green-966, light salmon-754, light blue-800, light green-913, light sea green-993, mint green-369, light gray green-504, lilac-211, light rosewood-761, light peach-951; 3 skeins middle blue-799; 2 skeins each salmon-352, salmon brown-758, light gray-762, rose-776; 1 skein each light blue gray-776, light moss green-472, bright rose-604, rosewood-760.
■ U.S. size 3 and 6 knitting needles. Circular needle U.S. size 3. (Metric sizes: 3.0, 4.0, and 3.0 circular.)

GAUGE
U.S. size 6 needles in St st: 4" (10 cm.) = 20 sts x 24 rows.
To save time, take time to check gauge!

BACK
With smaller size needles, cast on 94 (100, 106) sts and work 2-3/4" in 1/1 ribbing. Purl 1 row on wrong side of work, inc 16 (18, 20) sts evenly spaced across row = 110 (118, 126) sts.
Change to larger size needles, work in St st. Shape Armholes: When back measures 13-1/4" (13", 12-1/2") from beg, bind off 3 sts at beg of next 2 rows, bind off 2 sts at beg of next 2 rows = 100 (108, 116) sts.
Shape Neck: When back measures 9-1/4" (9-3/4", 10-1/4") from beg of arm-hole, bind off center 44 (46, 48) sts. Join 2nd ball of yarn to 2nd part and work at the same time. At each neck edge of every 2nd row, bind off 2 sts once, dec 1 st once.
Shape Shoulders: When back measures 10-1/4" (10-1/2", 11") from beg of armhole, bind off rem 25 (28, 31) sts on each shoulder.

FRONT
Beg front same as back.
Shape Neck: When front measures 8-1/2" (9", 9-1/4") from beg of armhole, bind off center 38 (40, 42) sts. Join 2nd ball of yarn to 2nd part and work at the same time. At each neck edge of every 2nd row, bind off 3 sts once, bind off 2 sts once, dec 1 st once.
Shape Shoulders: When front measures 10-1/4" (10-1/2", 11") from beg of arm-hole, bind off rem 25 (28, 31) sts on each shoulder.

SLEEVE
With smaller size needles, cast on 36 (40, 44) sts, work 2" in 1/1 ribbing. Purl 1 row on wrong side of work row, inc 22 (20, 18) sts evenly spaced across row = 58 (60, 62) sts.
Change to larger size needles, work in St st. Inc 1 st each edge of every 3rd row 1 (1, 5) times. Inc 1 st each edge of every 4th row 21 (22, 19) times. Work new sts in St st as you inc = 102 (106, 110) sts.
Shape Sleeve Top: When sleeve measures 17-1/4" from beg, bind off 3 sts at beg of next 2 rows, bind off 6 sts at beg of next 6 rows, bind off 7 sts at beg of next 6 rows, bind off rem 18 (22, 26) sts.

NECKBAND
Embroider the flowers in duplicate stitch on the body by foll chart, beg with point S1 (M1, L1). Center the chart for the sleeves at point M. Sew shoulder seams. With circular needle, pick up and knit 118 (122, 126) sts around neck. Work 1-1/4" in 1/1 ribbing, bind off.

FINISHING
Sew sleeves to side seams, matching center of sleeve to shoulder seam. Sew side and sleeve seams.

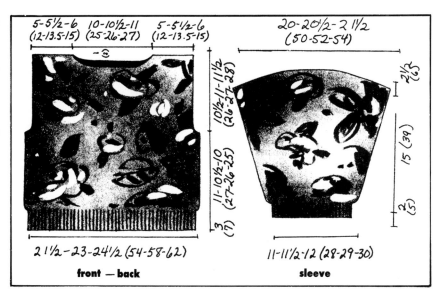

5-5½-6 10-10½-11 5-5½-6 (12-13.5-15) (25-26-27) (12-13.5-15)
20-20½-21½ (50-52-54)
10½-11-11½ (26-27-28)
11-10½-10 (27-26-25)
3 (7)
2½ (6.5)
15 (39)
2 (5)
21½-23-24½ (54-58-62)

front — back

11-11½-12 (28-29-30)

sleeve

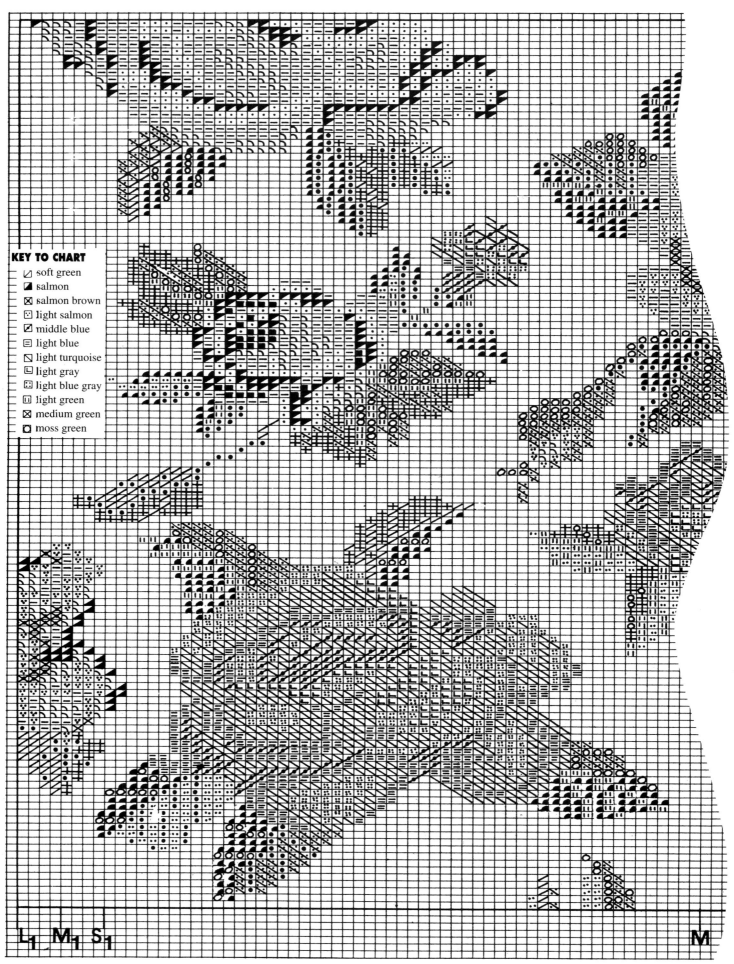

KEY TO CHART
◹ soft green
◢ salmon
⊠ salmon brown
⊡ light salmon
◪ middle blue
⊟ light blue
◺ light turquoise
⊔ light gray
⊡ light blue gray
⊞ light green
⊠ medium green
◐ moss green

L₁ M₁ S₁   M

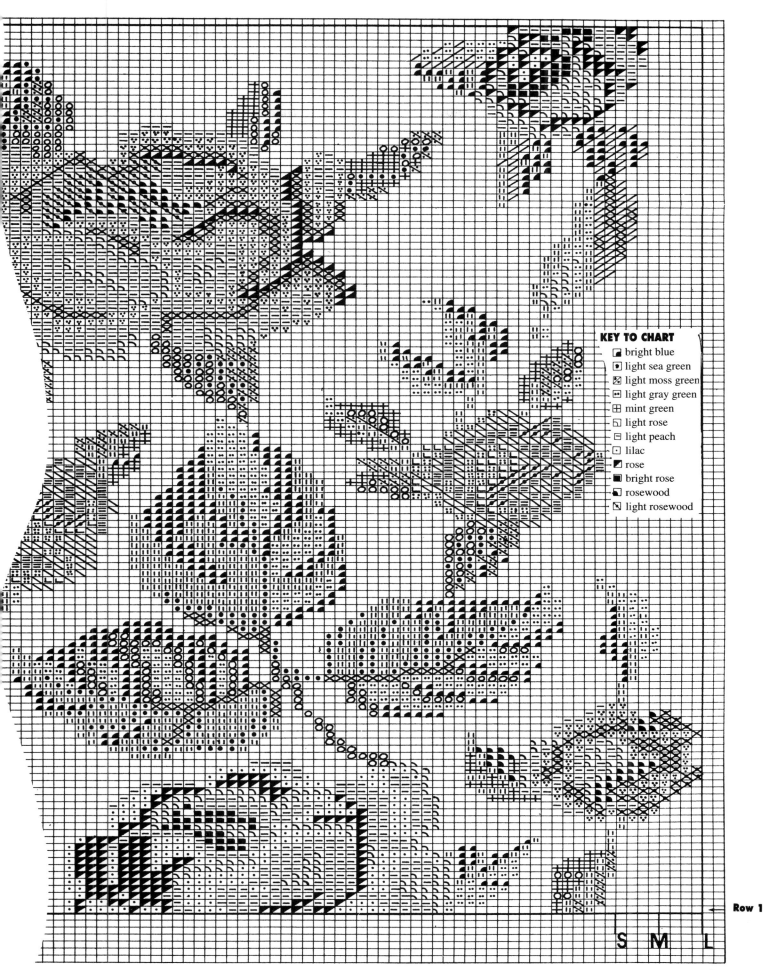

KEY TO CHART

- bright blue
- light sea green
- light moss green
- light gray green
- mint green
- light rose
- light peach
- lilac
- rose
- bright rose
- rosewood
- light rosewood

Row 1

S M L

Winter

RICH

✿✿✿ RICH

Eyelets and ruffles are accented by a rich border of embroidered roses.

SIZES
- Small (Medium, Large)
- Finished bust measurements: 44-1/2" (47-1/2", 51")
- Finished length: 27-1/2"
- Finished sleeve length: 18-3/4"

MATERIALS
- Scheepjeswol Invicta Extra (50 g): 10 (11, 12) balls red
- DMC Embroidery Floss: 1 skein each green-911, dark green-910, purple-552, light purple-554, bright fuchsia-814, fuchsia-816, red-817, dark rose-892, light rose-894, dark orange-946, rose-956, orange-3340, light orange-3341, róse red-3705
- U.S. size 1 and 2 knitting needles. 16" Circular needle U.S. size 1 and 2. (Metric sizes: 2.0, 2.5, and 2.5 40 cm. circular.)

GAUGE
U.S. size 2 needles in St st: 4" (10 cm.) = 30 sts x 39 rows.

To save time, take time to check gauge!

BACK
With larger size needles and Red, cast on 342 (366, 390) sts and knit 5 rows = 3 ridges, then work in St st until piece measures work 2-1/2" from beg. Work next wrong side row as foll: 1 border st, *k2 tog*, rep * to *, end with 1 border st = 172 (184, 196) sts. Continue in St st until piece measures 11-3/4" from beg. Work as foll: right side facing, 1 border st, 27 (28, 29) sts in St st, *11 sts in eyelet stitch foll chart, 10 (12, 14) sts in St st*, work * to * 6 times total, 17 (16, 15) sts in St st, 1 border st.
Shape Armholes: When back measures 16" (15-1/2", 15-1/4") from beg, bind off 4 sts at beg of next 2 rows. Bind off 3 sts at beg of next 4 rows. Bind off 2 sts at beg of next 6 rows. Dec 1 st at each edge of every 2nd row 4 times = 132 (144, 156) sts.
Shape Shoulders: When back measures 10-1/4" (10-1/2", 11") from beg of armhole, bind off 6 (7, 8) sts at beg of next 10 (6, 2) rows. Bind off 5 (6, 7) sts at beg of next 4 (8, 12) rows. **At the same time,** Shape Neck: When back measures 26-3/4" from beg, bind off center 34 (36, 38) sts. Join 2nd ball of yarn to 2nd part and work at the same. At each neck edge of every 2nd row, bind off 4 sts once, bind off 3 sts once, bind off 2 sts once.

FRONT
Beg front same as back. Shape armholes as on back.
Shape Neck: When front measures 8-1/2" (9", 9-1/4") from beg of armhole, bind off center 10 (12, 14) sts. Join 2nd ball of yarn to 2nd part and work at the same time. At each neck edge of every 2nd row, bind off 4 sts once, bind off 3 sts twice, bind off 2 sts 3 times, dec 1 st 5 times.
Shape Shoulders: When front measures 10-1/4" (10-1/2", 11") from beg of armhole, shape shoulders as on back.

SLEEVE
With larger size needles and Red, cast on 58 (60, 62) sts, knit 5 rows = 3 ridges, then continue in St st until piece measures 5" from beg. Inc 1 st each edge of every 2nd row 20 (24, 28) times. Inc 1 st each edge of every 4th row 22 (20, 18) times. Work new sts in St st as you inc = 142 (148, 154) sts. When sleeve measures 18-3/4" from beg, end wrong side of work row.
Shape Sleeve Top: Bind off 4 sts at beg of next 2 rows. Bind off 3 sts at beg of next 4 rows. Bind off 2 sts at beg of next 30 rows. Bind off 3 sts at beg of next 4 rows. Bind off 4 (4,

5) sts at beg of next 4 rows. Bind off 6 (7, 7) sts at beg of next 4 rows. Bind off rem 10 (12, 14) rows.

FINISHING

Trace the flower motif on a piece of tissue paper and pin pattern to lower front. Run a basting thread along the stems and along the outside edges of the flowers and leaves. Remove the tissue paper and embroider the stems in stem stitch in dark green and the leaves in green and flowers in satin stitch in indicated colors. Use the sketch and photo as a guide. Embroider the back the same.

Sew shoulder seams. Neckband: With larger size circular needle and Red, pick up and knit 128 (132, 136) sts around neck and work in St st. Work 3/4" with larger size circular needle, then change to smaller size needles and work 1", change to larger size needle and work 3/4".

Bind off. Fold neckband to inside and slip stitch in place. Set in sleeves, matching center of sleeve to shoulder seam. Sew side and sleeve seams.

KEY TO CHART

☐ K1 on right side of work rows, p1 on wrong side of work rows

◢ K2 tog

◣ Sl 1, k1, PSSO

⊡ yo

NOTE: Chart shows right side of work rows only. Purl wrong side of work rows, purling the yos.

EMBROIDERY

1 = purple - 552
2 = light purple - 554
3 = bright fuchsia - 814
4 = fuchsia - 816
5 = red - 817
6 = dark rose - 892
7 = light rose -894,
8 = dark orange - 946
9 = rose - 956
10 = orange -3340
11 = light orange -3341
12 = rose red - 3705

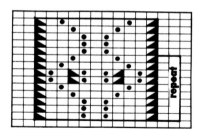

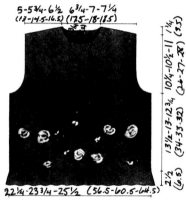

5-5¾-6½ 6¼-7-7¼
(13-14.5-16.5) (17.5-18-18.5)

13½-13-12¾ 10¼-10½-11 1¼
(34-33-32) (26-27-28) (3.5)

2½
(6.5)

22¼-23¾-25½ (56.5-60.5-64.5)

front — back

18¼-19-20 (46.5-48.5-50.5)

5
(13)

13¾
(35)

5
(13)

7¼-7¾-8 (18.5-19.5-20)

sleeve

❀ JUBILANT
❀❀

Jubilant Spring flowers

on a Winter-white

pullover represent the

best of both seasons.

SIZES
■ Small (Medium, Large)
■ Finished bust measurements: 42" (44-1/2", 47")
■ Finished length: 27-1/2"
■ Finished sleeve length: 17-3/4"

MATERIALS
■ Stahl Lima (50 g): 12 (13, 13) balls Winter White
■ DMC embroidery floss: 3 skeins lilac-209, 4 skeins light lilac-211, 3 skeins gray-318, 1 skein purple-550, 3 skeins dark green-561, 3 skeins green-562, 10 skeins light green-564, 3 skeins rose-603, 5 skeins light rose-605, small amounts: old rose and light old rose.
■ U.S. size 4 and 6 knitting needles. 16" Circular needle U.S. size 4. (Metric sizes: 3.5, 4.0, and 3.5 40 cm. circular.)

GAUGE
U.S. size 6 needles in St st: 4" (10 cm.) = 19 sts x 25 rows.
To save time, take time to check gauge!

BACK
With smaller size needles and Winter White, cast on 94 (98, 102) sts and work 2-3/4" in 2/2 ribbing as foll: 1 border st, k1, *p2, k2*, rep * to * across, end with p2, k1, 1 border st. Purl 1 row across wrong side of work, inc 10 (11, 13) sts evenly spaced across row = 104 (109, 115) sts.
Change to larger size needles, work in St st.
Shape Armholes: When back measures 17-3/4" (17-1/4", 17") - 94 (92, 90) rows from beg, bind off 2

sts at beg of next 4 rows. Dec 1 st at each edge of every 2nd row once = 94 (99, 105) sts.
Shape Neck: When back measures 9" (9-1/4", 9-3/4") from beg of armhole, bind off center 28 (29, 31) sts. Join 2nd ball of yarn to 2nd part and work at the same time. At each neck edge of every 2nd row, 3 sts once.
Shape Shoulders: When back measures 9-3/4" (10-1/4", 10-1/2") from beg of armhole - 158 rows above ribbing, bind off rem 30 (32, 34) sts on each shoulder.

FRONT
Beg front same as back.
Shape Armholes as on on back.
Shape Neck: When front measures 7-1/2" (8", 8-1/4") from beg of armhole, bind off center 14 (15, 17) sts. Join 2nd ball of yarn to 2nd part and work at the same time. At each neck

edge of every 2nd row, 3 sts once, bind off 2 sts twice, dec 1 st 3 times.
Shape Shoulders: When front measures 9-3/4" (10-1/4", 10-1/2") from beg of armhole - 158 rows above border, bind off rem 30 (32, 34) sts on each shoulder.

SLEEVE
With smaller size needles and Winter White, cast on 38 (42, 42) sts, work 2-1/2" in 1/1 ribbing. Purl 1 row on wrong side, inc 9 (7, 9) sts evenly spaced across = 47 (49, 51) sts. Change to larger size needles, work in St st. Inc 1 st each edge of every 2nd row 1 (3, 5) times. Inc 1 st each edge of every 4th row 22 (21, 20) times. Work new sts in St st as you inc = 93 (97, 101) sts.
When sleeve measures 17-3/4"-98 rows above border, end wrong side of work row.
Shape Sleeve Top: Bind off 2 sts at beg of next 4

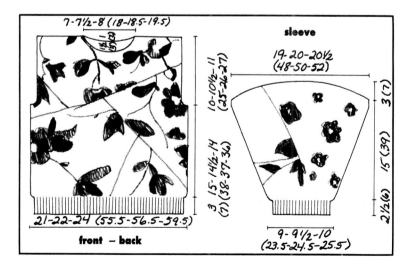

front – back

sleeve

7-7½-8 (18-18.5-19.5)

10-10½-11 (25-26-27)

3 15-14½-14 (7) (38-37-36)

21-22-24 (55.5-56.5-59.5)

19-20-20½ (48-50-52)

3 (7)

15 (39)

2½ (6)

9-9½-10 (23.5-24.5-25.5)

rows. Bind off 3 sts at beg of next 6 rows. Bind off 6 sts at beg of next 6 rows. Bind off 7 (8, 9) sts at beg of next 2 rows. Bind off rem 17 (19, 21) sts.

FINISHING
Embroider front in duplicate stitch by foll chart 1 as foll: 1 border st, then work from point 1 (2, 3) to point 4 (5, 6), end with 1 border st. Embroider back by scattering flowers as you desire foll chart 2. Embroider left sleeve centering chart 3 on sleeve cap and right sleeve centering chart 4. Scatter flowers on both sleeves foll chart 2. Use photo as a guide. Sew shoulder seams. With circular needle and Winter White, pick up and knit 108 (112, 116) sts around neck. Work 2-1/2" in 2/2 ribbing, bind off. Set in sleeves, matching center of sleeve to shoulder seam, taking care to match gray line on front with gray line on sleeve. Sew side and sleeve seams.

Chart 2

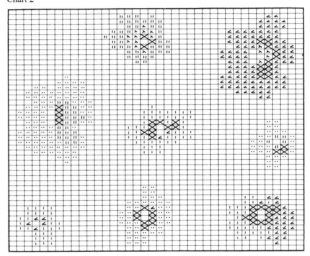

Chart 3

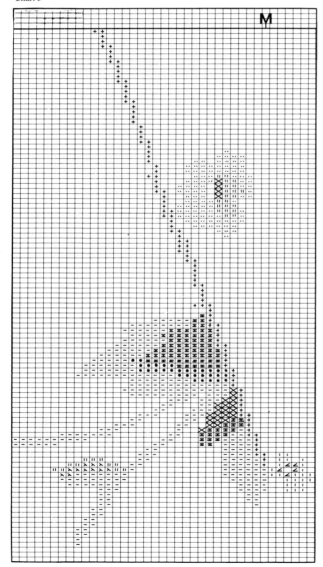

Chart 4

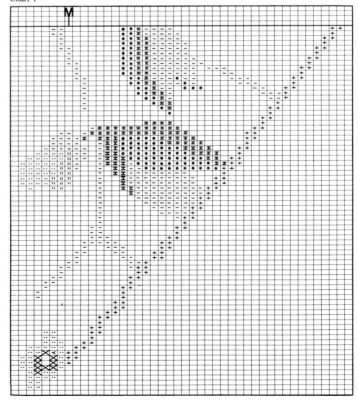

KEY TO CHART

- ⊠ dark green
- ⊡ green
- ⊟ light green
- ⊡ light rose
- ⊞ rose
- ⊠ old rose
- ⊠ purple
- ⊡ light lilac
- ⊠ lilac
- ⊞ gray

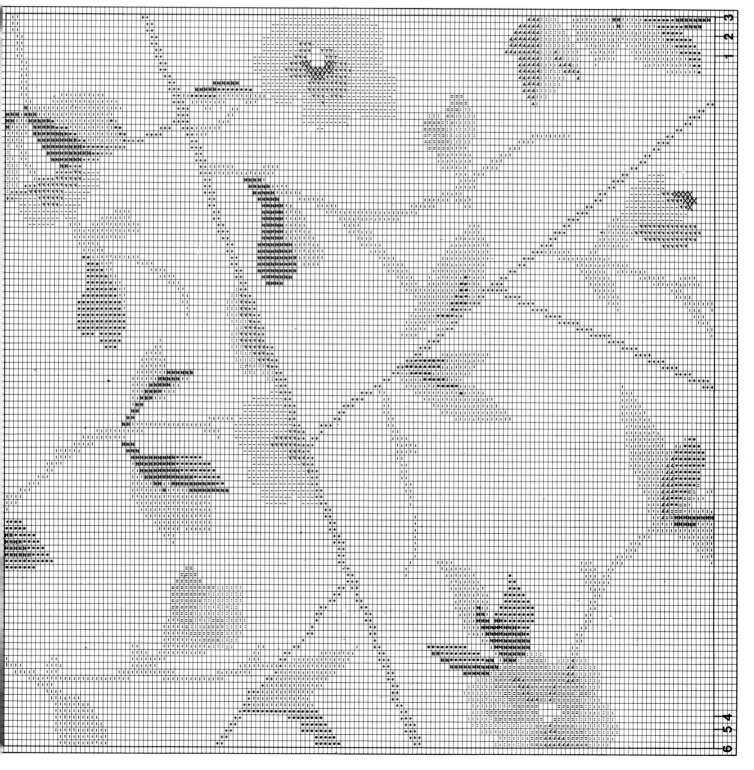

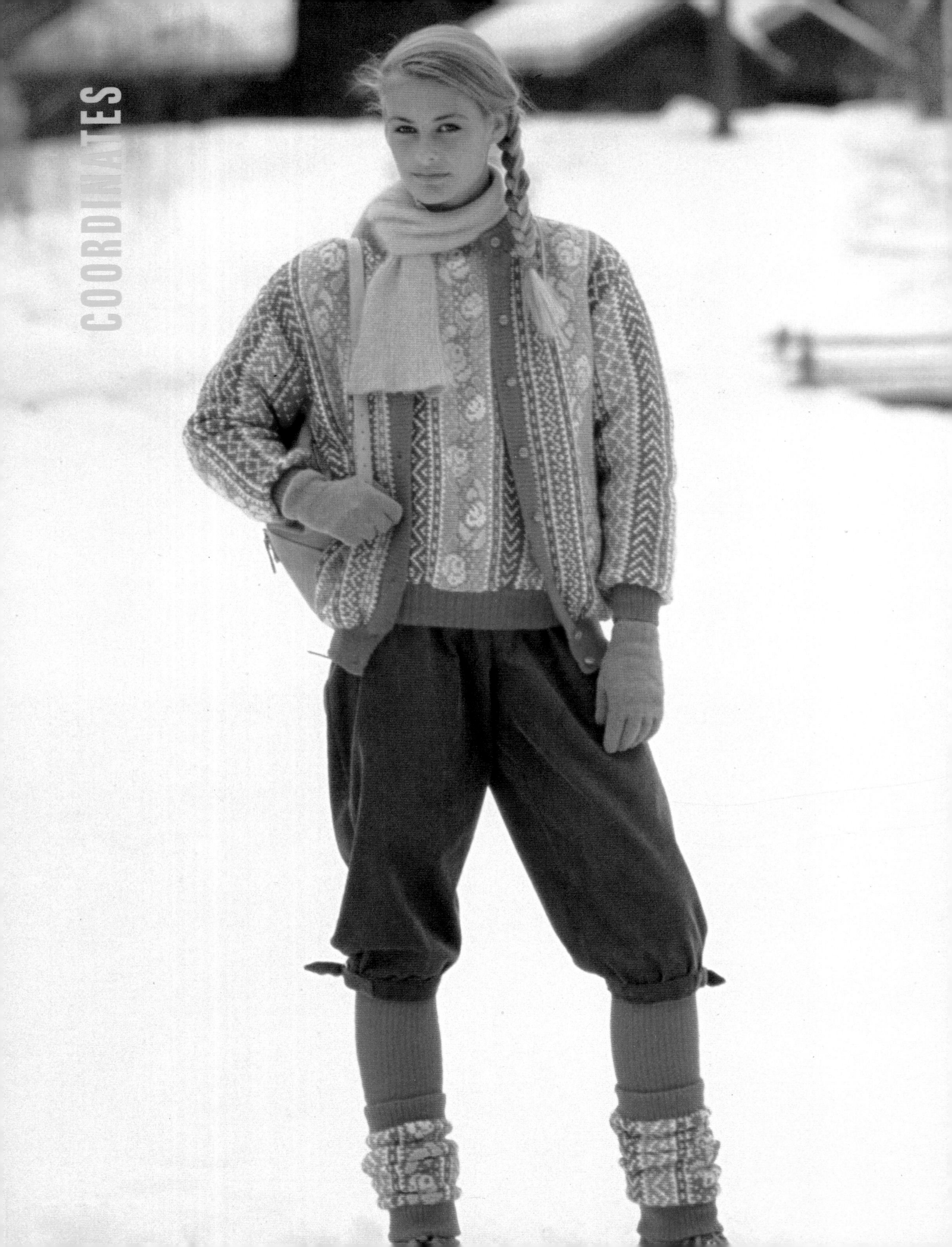

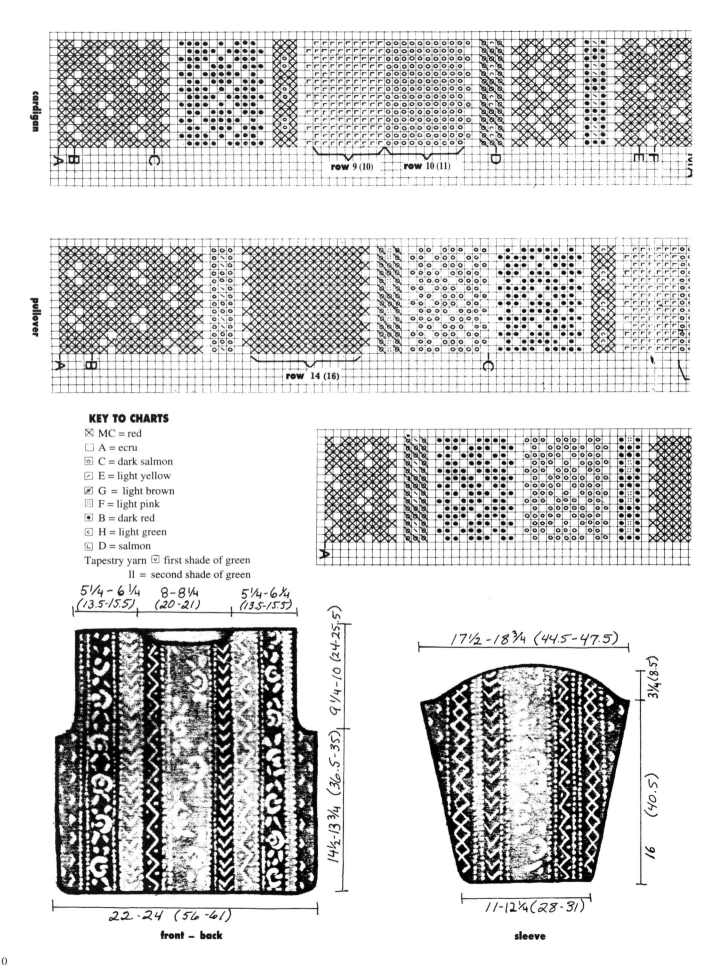

cardigan

A B C row 9 (10) row 10 (11) D E F

pullover

A row 14 (16) C

KEY TO CHARTS

⊠ MC = red
☐ A = ecru
⊡ C = dark salmon
☑ E = light yellow
⊠ G = light brown
⊞ F = light pink
⊡ B = dark red
☐ H = light green
☐ D = salmon
Tapestry yarn ☑ first shade of green
      ll = second shade of green

A

5¼ - 6¼ (13.5-15.5)   8-8¼ (20-21)   5¼-6¼ (13.5-15.5)

9¼-10 (24-25.5)

14½-13¾ (36.5-35)

22·24 (56-61)

front – back

17½-18¾ (44.5-47.5)

3¼ (8.5)

16 (40.5)

11-12¼ (28-31)

sleeve

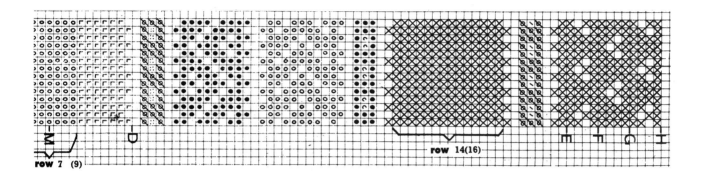

row 10 (11) — row 9 (10)

row 7 (9)

row 14(16)

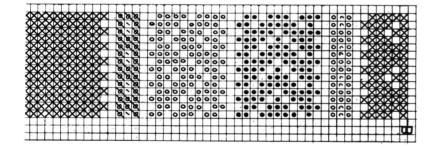

Embroider the leaves and flowers in colors as you desire.

Wide Flower Band

—M

Narrow Flower Band

—M

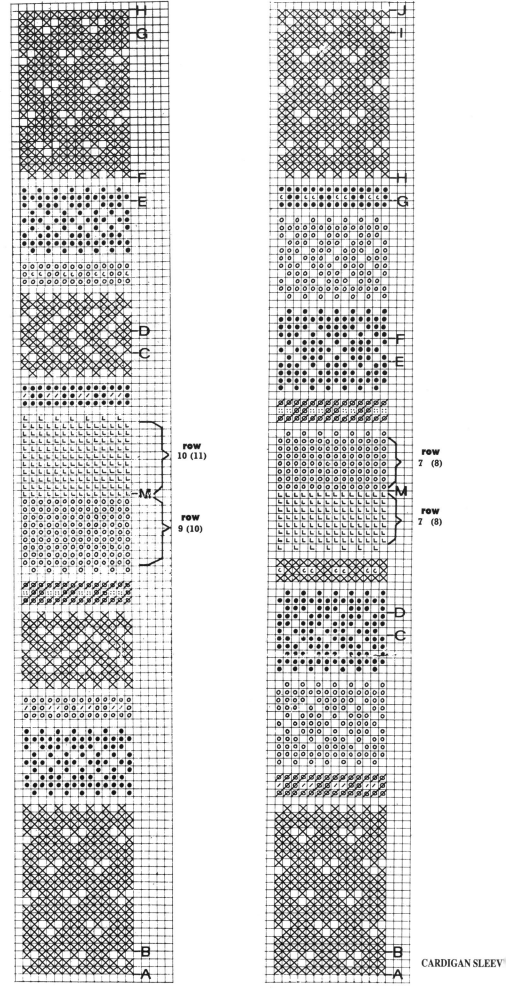

row
10 (11)

row
9 (10)

row
7 (8)

row
7 (8)

PULLOVER SLEEVE

CARDIGAN SLEEV

FLAIR

⚙ FLAIR

South America's flair for design is showcased in this child's pullover.

SIZES
■ 4 (6, 7) years
■ Finished chest measurements: 27-1/2" (29", 30-3/4")
■ Finished length: 16-1/4" (18-1/4", 20")
■ Finished sleeve length: 11" (12-1/4", 13-1/4")

MATERIALS
■ Scheepjeswol Invicta Extra (50 g): 3 balls Blue - MC; 2 (3, 3) balls Ecru - A; 1 ball Black - B
■ Linen yarn (50 g) 187 yds per 50 g skein: 3 (4, 4) balls Blue - C; 2 (2, 3) balls White - D; 1 ball Black - E
■ DMC embroidery floss: your choice of heather shades to embroider over lower band on body and sleeves.
■ U.S. size 2 and 4 knitting needles. Circular needle U.S. size 2. (Metric sizes: 2.5 and 3.5.)

GAUGE
U.S. size 4 needles in St st using 1 strand of Invicta Extra and 1 strand of linen together: 4" (10 cm.) = 24 sts x 27 rows.
To save time, take time to check gauge!

BACK
With larger size needles and 1 strand each MC and C, cast on 86 (91, 96) sts and work in fairisle St st foll chart 1 as foll: 1 border st, work from point 1 (2, 3) to point 4 (5, 6), 1 border st. Last row on chart is worked on right side of work. Carry unused yarns loosely across wrong side of work. Use 1 strand of wool and 1 strand of linen together. Continue by foll chart 2. Knit first row on wrong side of work. Beg chart with 1 border st, then

point 1 (2, 3) to point 4 (5, 6) and work to point A (B, C) on chart, 1 border st vertically - 11" (12-1/2", 13-3/4") from beg.
Shape Armholes: Bind off 2 sts at beg of next 2 rows, dec 1 st each edge of every 2nd row once = 80 (85, 90) sts.
Shape Shoulders: When back measures 6-1/2" (7", 7-1/2") from beg of armhole - point D (E, F) on chart, at each armhole edge of every 2nd row, bind off 8 (8, 9) sts 2 (3, 1) time, bind off 7 (0, 8) sts 1 (0, 2) times. When back measures 18-1/2" (20-1/2", 22") from beg - point G (H, I) on chart, place rem 34 (37, 40) sts on holder for neck.

FRONT
Beg front same as back. Shape Neck and Shoulders: When front measures 6" (6 -1/4", 6-1/2") from beg of armhole, bind off center 14 (17, 20) sts. Join 2nd ball of yarn to 2nd part and work at the same time. At each neck edge of every 2nd row, bind off 4 sts once, bind off 3 sts once, bind off 2 sts once, dec 1 st once. At the same time, at each armhole edge of every 2nd row, bind off 8 (8, 9) sts 2 (3, 1) time, bind off 7 (0, 8) sts 1 (0, 2) times.

SLEEVE
With larger size needles and 1 strand each MC and C, cast on 59 (62, 64) sts, work in fairisle St st centering charts at point M1 (M, M). At the same time, inc 1 st each edge of every 4th row 2 (1, 0) time. Inc 1 st each edge of every 6th row 8 (10, 12) times. Work new sts in fairisle St st as

you inc = 79 (84, 88) sts.
Shape Sleeve Top: When sleeve measures 13-1/4" (14-1/2", 15-1/4") from beg, bind off 3 sts at beg of next 2 rows, bind off 4 (5, 5) sts at beg of next 2 rows, bind off 6 (6, 7) sts at beg of next 2 rows, bind off 9 sts at beg of next 2 rows. Bind off rem 35 (38, 40) sts.

NECKBAND
With larger size needle and 1 strand each MC and C, pick up and knit 34 (37, 40) sts from back neck and cast on 1 st at each edge for border st. Work in fairisle St st centering chart 3. Work neckband so that right side of work is on inside (will be folded to outside). 1 st in from right edge of every 2nd row, k2 tog, work to last 3 sts, k2 tog through back loop, 1 border st. Work to point A on chart, then inc 1 st at each edge of every 2nd row by knitting 1 st in the strand between the border sts and the adjacent st. After the last row of chart, bind off. Work same border on front, picking up 40 (43, 46) sts on front neck and casting on 1 st at each edge for border st.

FINISHING
Sew shoulder and neckband seams. Fold neckband in half to outside and blind stitch in place. Set in sleeves, matching center of sleeve to shoulder seam. Sew side and sleeve seams. Fold all borders to inside and slip stitch in place. Embroider the ecru stripe in duplicate stitch in colors you desire using photo as a guide.

KEY TO CHART
⊟ 1 strand of MC and 1 strand of C
☐ 1 strand of A and 1 strand of D
⊡ 1 strand of B and 1 strand of E

Chart 3

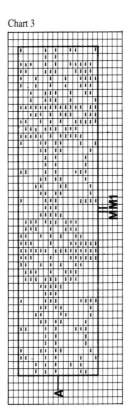

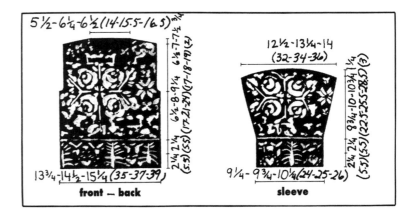

5½ - 6¼ - 6½ (14·15.5·16.5)
12½-13¼-14 (32-34-36)
13¾-14½-15¼ (35-37-39)
9¼ - 9¾-10¼ (24-25-26)

front — back

sleeve

Chart 1

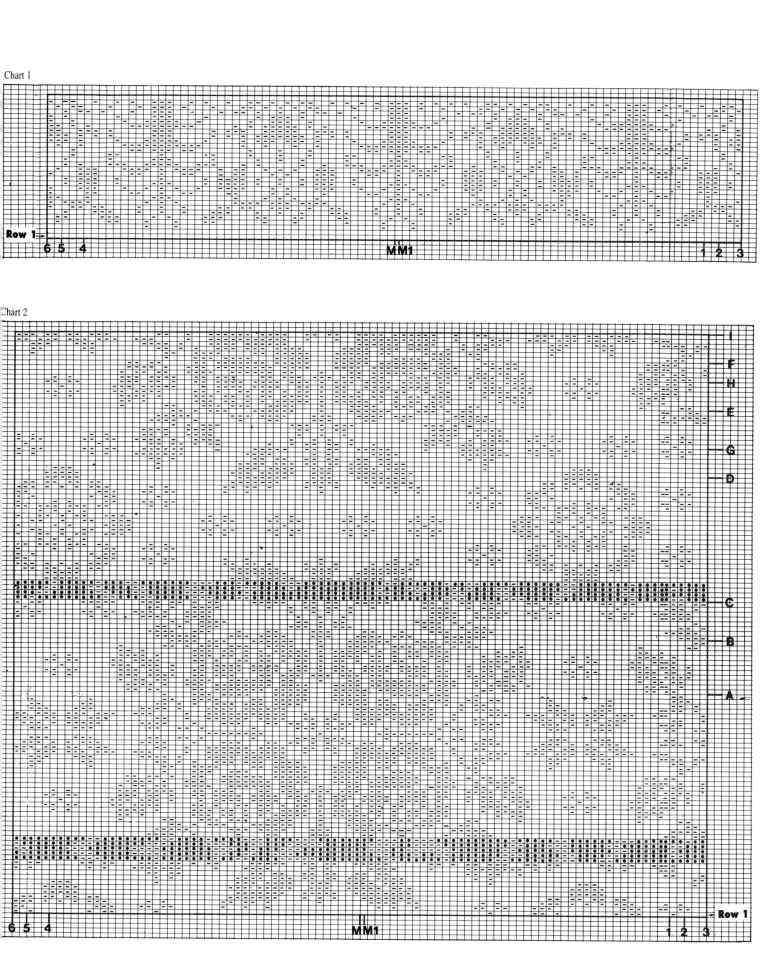

Row 1

6 5 4   MM1   1 2 3

Chart 2

6 5 4   MM1   Row 1   1 2 3

SPORTY

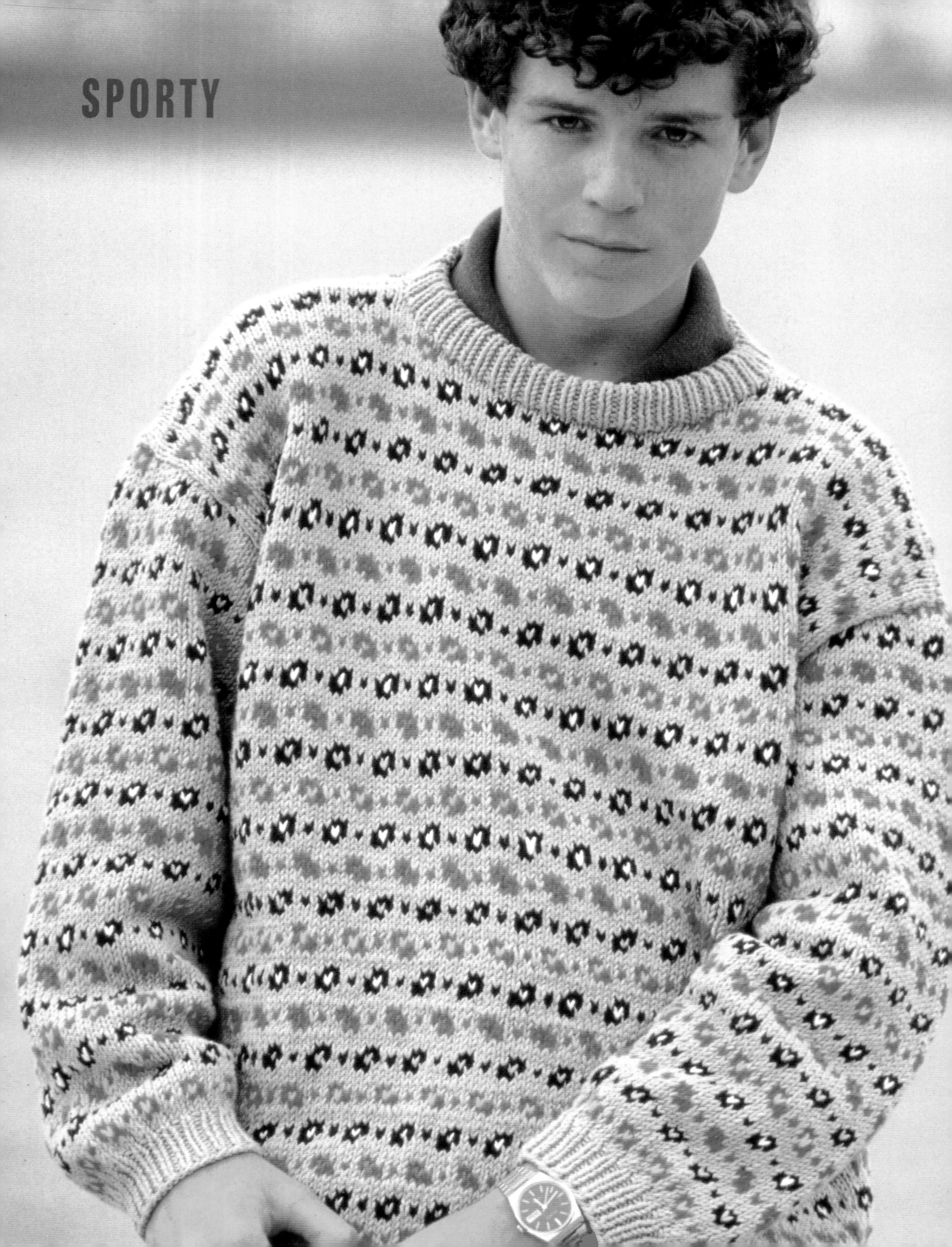

❀ SPORTY

Abstract flower motif

stripes make a sporty

statement for men.

SIZES
- Small (Medium, Large)
- Finished chest measurements: 42-1/2" (45", 47")
- Finished length: 24-3/4"
- Finished sleeve length: 17-3/4"

MATERIALS
- Mayflower Helarsgarn (50 g): 15 (16, 16) balls Khaki - MC; 2 balls each Black - A and Red - B; 1 ball each Orange Red - C, Yellow - D, Dark Gray - E and Brown - F
- U.S. size 5 and 7 knitting needles. Circular needle U.S. size 5. (Metric sizes: 3.75 and 4.5.)

GAUGE
U.S. size 7 needles in fairisle St st: 4" = 19 sts x 22 rows.
U.S. size 7 needles in St st: 4" (10 cm.) = 19 sts x 26 rows.
To save time, take time to check gauge!

BACK
With smaller size needles and MC, cast on 88 (92, 96) sts and work 1-1/2" in 1/1 ribbing. Purl 1 row on wrong side of work, inc 16 (18, 20) sts evenly spaced across row = 104 (110, 116) sts.
Change to larger size needles, work in fairisle St st foll chart. Beg with 1 border st, then work from point A to B 17 (18,19) times, end with 1 border st. Carry unused yarn loosely across wrong side of work.
Shape Armholes: When back measures 15-3/4" (15-1/4", 15") from beg, bind off 3 sts at beg of next 2 rows, bind off 2 sts at beg of next 2 rows, dec 1 st at each edge of every 2nd row once = 92 (98, 104) sts.

When back measures 9" (9-1/4", 9-3/4") from beg of armhole, end with 10th row of pattern stitch = 6-1/2 vertical repeats, bind off all sts.

FRONT
Beg front same as back. Shape Neck: When front measures 22-1/2" from beg, bind off center 24 (26, 28) sts. Join 2nd ball of yarn to 2nd part and work at the same time. At each neck edge of every 2nd row. bind off 3 sts once, bind off 2 sts once, dec 1 st once.
When front measures 9" (9-1/4", 9-3/4") from beg of armhole—end same row as back, bind off rem 28 (30, 32) sts on each shoulder.

SLEEVE
With smaller size needles and MC, cast on 42 (44, 46) sts, work 1-1/2" in 1/1 ribbing. Purl 1 row on wrong side of work, inc 14 (14, 16) sts evenly spaced across row = 56 (58, 62) sts.
Change to larger size needles, work in fairisle St st foll chart. Beg 1 border st, point A (C, D) and end with Point B (E, F) on chart, end with 1 border st. Inc 1 st each edge of every 6th row 12 (10, 8) times. Inc 1 st each edge of every 4th row 3 (6, 8) times. Work new sts in fairisle St st as you inc = 86 (90, 94) sts.
Shape Sleeve Top: When sleeve measures 17-3/4" from beg, bind off 4 sts at beg of next 2 rows, bind off 5 sts at beg of next 2 rows, bind off 6 sts at beg of next 4 rows, bind off 7 sts at beg of next 4 rows, bind off rem 16 (20, 24) sts.

NECKBAND
Sew shoulder seams. With circular needle and MC, pick up and knit 86 (90, 94) sts around neck. Work 2" in 1/1 ribbing, bind off. Fold in half to inside and slip stitch in place.

FINISHING
Set in sleeves. Sew side and sleeve seams.

KEY TO CHART
- □ = MC
- ⊡ = E
- ⊟ = B
- ⊡ = D
- ⊡ = C
- ⊙ = A
- ⧄ = F

FAIRISLE CHART

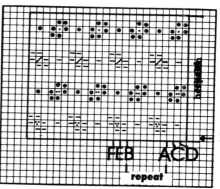

Row 1

FEB ACD

repeat

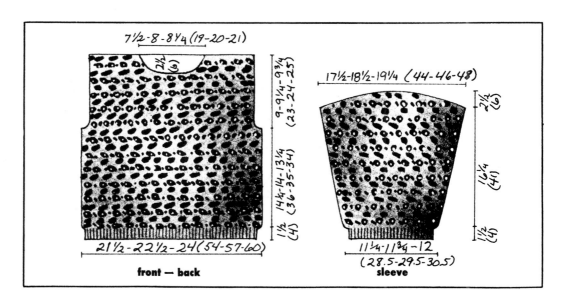

7½-8-8¾ (19-20-21)

9-9¼-9¾ (23-24-25)

14¼-14-13¾ (36-35-34)

2½ (6)

1½ (4)

21½-22½-24(54-57-60)

front — back

17½-18½-19¼ (44-46-48)

2½ (6)

16¼ (41)

1½ (4)

11¼-11¾-12 (28.5-29.5-30.5)

sleeve

COZY

CHART 1

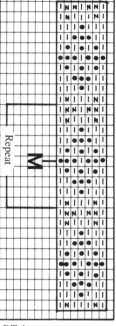

❀❀ COZY
❀❀❀
❀

Embroidered and knit-in

motifs of tulips, narcissus,

and windmills are the

perfect companions on

these pullovers..

SIZES
■ 8 (10, 12) years
■ Finished chest measurements: 31" (32", 33")
■ Finished length: 20-3/4" (21-1/2", 22-1/2")
■ Finished sleeve length: 13-3/4" (14-1/4", 15")

MATERIALS
■ Mayflower Cotton 8 (50 g): 5 (5, 6) balls Rose - MC; 2 balls White - A; 1 ball each Red - B, Blue - C, Turquoise - D, Green - E, Light Green - F, Yellow - G and Black - H
■ U.S. size 2 and 3 knitting needles. 24" Circular needles U.S. size 2 and 3. (Metric sizes: 2.5, 3.0, and 2.5 and 3.0 60 cm. circular.)

GAUGE
U.S. size 3 needles in St st:

4" (10 cm.) = 26 sts x 36 rows.
To save time, take time to check gauge!

BACK
With smaller size needles and B, cast on 90 (92, 94) sts and work 2" in 1/1 ribbing. Purl 1 row on wrong side of work, inc 15 (17, 17) sts evenly spaced across row = 105 (109, 111) sts.
Change to larger size needles, work in dot st as foll: 1 border st, then work chart 1: work from point 1 to point 2, 25 (26, 27) times and point 2 to point 3 (3, 4) once, 1 border st. Carry unused yarn loosely across wrong side of work. Work until back measures 20-3/4" (21-1/2", 22-1/2") from beg, bind off all sts.

FRONT
Beg front same as back. Change to larger size circular needle and MC, working back and forth, work 4 (5, 6) rows in MC, 7 rows in A, 3 (4, 5) rows in MC, 153 rows foll chart 2, complete in MC. Beg and end all charts with 1 border st and work from point 1 (2, 3) to point 4 (5, 6), 1 border st. Beg at the end of the needle where the necessary color hangs. Use a separate ball of yarn for each section of color. Be sure to cross yarns on wrong side of work when changing colors.
Shape Neck: When front measures 18-3/4" (19-3/4", 20-1/2") - point A (B, C) on chart, bind off center 23 (25, 27) sts. Join 2nd ball of yarn to 2nd shoulder and work at the same time. At each neck edge of every 2nd row, bind off 4 sts once, bind off 2 sts twice, dec 1 st 3 times.
Shape Shoulders: When front measures 20-3/4"(21-1/2", 22-1/2") from beg - 173 (180, 187) rows above border, bind off rem 30 (31, 31) sts on each shoulder.

SLEEVE
With smaller size needles and B, cast on 50 (52, 54) sts, work 1-1/2" in 1/1 ribbing. Purl 1 row on wrong side of work, inc 9 (9, 8) sts evenly spaced across row = 59 (61, 62) sts.
Change to larger size needles, work in St st as foll: 9 (9, 10) rows MC, 1 row A,

1 row C, 11 rows A, 1 row C, 1 row A, 15 (16, 17) rows MC, 9 rows A, 23 (25, 27) rows MC, 1 row A, 1 row B, 19 rows A, 1 row B, 1 row A, complete in MC. **At the same time,** inc 1 st each edge of every 4th row 12 (7, 10) times. Inc 1 st each edge of every 6th row 9 (13, 12) times. Work new sts in St st as you inc = 101 (101, 106) sts.
When sleeve measures 13-3/4" (14-1/4", 15") from beg, bind off all sts.

NECKBAND
Embroider pieces in duplicate st foll chart 2. On the white rows, work centering chart 3 at lower edge of body, then center charts 4 (5, 6) on sleeves, centering at point M (M, M1) using the photo as a guide. Sew shoulder seams. With smaller size circular needle and D, pick up and knit 114 (118, 122) sts around neck. Work 1-1/4" in 1/1 ribbing, bind off.

FINISHING
Sew sleeves to side seams, matching center of sleeve to shoulder seam. Sew side and sleeve seams.

KEY TO CHARTS 1, 3, 4, & 5
□ = MC
⊠ = E
⊡ = B
⊙ = C
⊡ = G
⊟ = A

CHART 3

CHART 4

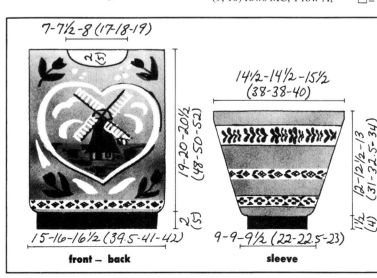

7-7½-8 (17-18-19)

19-20-20½ (48-50-52)

14½-14½-15½ (38-38-40)

12-12½-13 (31-32.5-34)

2 (5)

1½ (4)

15-16-16½ (39.5-41-42)

front – back

9-9-9½ (22-22.5-23)

sleeve

KEY TO CHART2

- ⊡ = D
- ☐ = MC
- ⊠ = E
- ⊡ = B
- ⊡ = C
- ⊡ = G
- ✳ = H
- ⊟ = A
- ⊡ = F

CHART 5

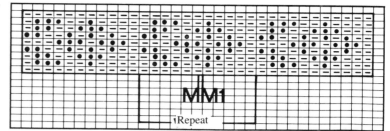

ART 2

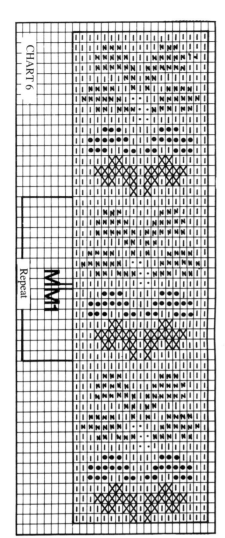

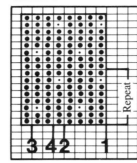

CHART 1

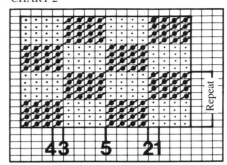

CHART 2

3 4 2 1

4 3 5 2 1

**KEY TO CHARTS
1 & 2**
- ⊡ A
- ⊙ MC
- ▨ D

CHART 3

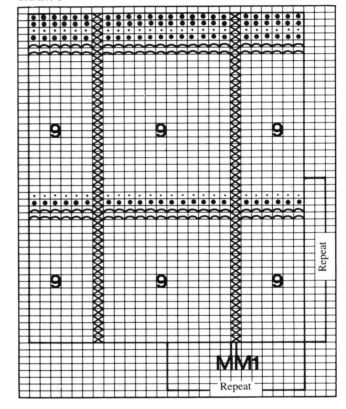

9 9 9

9 9 9

MM1

Repeat

CHILD'S PULLOVER

SIZES
- ■ 10 (12, 14) years
- ■ Finished chest measurements: 32" (34-1/2", 36-1/2")
- ■ Finished length: 21-1/2" (23-1/4", 24-3/4")
- ■ Finished sleeve length: 14-1/4" (15-1/2", 16-3/4")

MATERIALS
- ■ Mayflower Cotton 8 (50 g): 6 (7, 7) balls Blue - MC; 2 balls White - A; 1 ball each Rose - B, Yellow - C, Turquoise - D, Green - E, Red - F, Gray - G, Black - H and Orange - I
- ■ U.S. size 2 and 3 knitting needles. 24" Circular needle U.S. size 2 and 3. Crochet hook U.S. size C/2. (Metric sizes: 2.5, 3.0, and 2.5 and 3.0 60 cm. circular; 3.0 crochet hook.)

GAUGE
U.S. size 3 needles in St st dot: 4" (10 cm.) = 26 sts x 36 rows.

U.S. size 3 needles in block st: 4" (10 cm.) = 30 sts x 38 rows.
To save time, take time to check gauge!

BACK
With smaller size needles and MC, cast on 92 (96, 102) sts and work 1-1/2" (2", 2") in 1/1 ribbing. Purl 1 row on wrong side of work, inc 17 (19, 21) sts evenly spaced across row = 109 (115, 123) sts. Change to larger size circular needle, working back and forth, work in dot st by foll chart 1, beg with 1 border st, then point 1 to point 2, 26 (28, 30) times and point 2 to point 3 (4, 4) once, 1 border st. Beg at the end of the row where the necessary yarn hangs. Carry unused yarn loosely across wrong side of work. When back measures 21-1/2" (23-1/4", 24-3/4") from beg, bind off all sts.

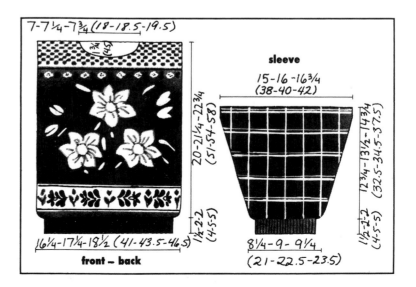

7-7¼-7¾ (18-18.5-19.5)

sleeve

15-16-16¾ (38-40-42)

20-2¼-22¾ (51-54-58)

12¾-13½-14¾ (32.5-34.5-37.5)

1½-2-2 (4-5-5)

16¼-17¼-18½ (41-43.5-46.5)

front – back

8¼-9-9¼ (21-22.5-23.5)

KEY TO CHARTS 3, 4, & 6

◻ with dot = A
◻ with dash = E
◻ with = = F
◻ with / = D

◉ = MC
◻ = C
x = rev St st

KEY TO CHART 5

• or 8 = A
– = E
= = F
● or 9 = MC
v = B

■ = H
◻ = C
z = I
/ = G

CHART 4

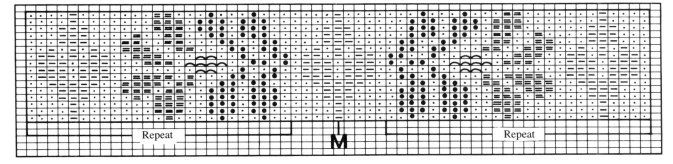

CHART 5

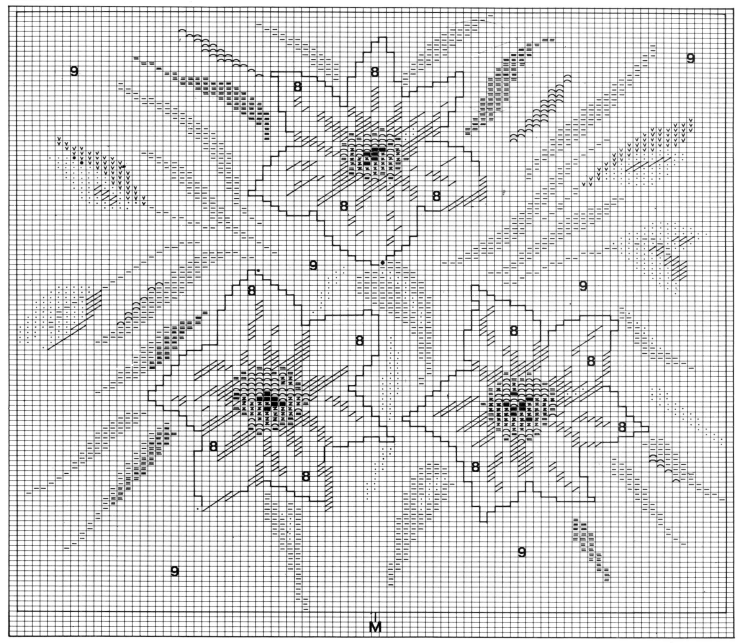

FRONT

Beg front same as back, but above ribbing work as foll: 3 (7, 11) rows in D, 1 row A, 2 rows F, 20 rows A, 2 rows F, 1 row A, 131 (131, 133) rows MC, 2 rows F, *2 rows A, 20 (28, 36) rows foll chart 2 - 184 (196, 210) rows total. On the first row of A after the *, inc 15 (17, 19) sts = 124 (132, 142) sts, then work in block pat as foll: 1 border st, work chart 2 from point 1 to point 2, 1 (1, 0) time and point 2 to point 3, 15 (16, 17) times and point 3 (3, 2) to point 4 (4, 5) once, 1 border st. Work 3 (11, 19) rows of chart 2, then

Shape Neck: Bind off center 34 (36, 38) sts. Join 2nd ball of yarn to 2nd shoulder and work at the same time. At each neck edge of every 2nd row, bind off 3 sts once, bind off 2 sts twice, dec 1 st 3 times. Shape Shoulders: When front measures 21-1/2" (23-1/4", 24-3/4") from beg, bind off rem 35 (38, 42) sts on each shoulder.

SLEEVE

With smaller size needles and B, cast on 44 (46, 48) sts, work 1-1/2" (2", 2") in 1/1 ribbing. Purl 1 row on wrong side of work, inc 13 (14, 14) sts evenly spaced across last row = 57 (60, 63) sts.
Change to larger size circular needle, working back and forth in striped pat, center chart 3 at M1 (M, M1). **At the same time,** inc 1 st each edge of every 4th row 12 (12, 10) times. Inc 1 st each edge of every 6th row 10 (11, 14) times. Work new sts in striped pat as you inc = 101 (106, 111) sts.
When sleeve measures 14-1/4" (15-1/2", 16-3/4") from beg, bind off all sts.

FINISHING

Embroider pieces in duplicate st foll charts. Over the lower rows in A, center chart 4, beg on the 3rd row of A. Embroider 131 (131, 133) rows of MC by foll chart 5, beg on the 2nd (2nd, 3rd) row of MC. Embroider foll chart 6, beg embroidery on the 8th row in MC by centering chart at M. With crochet hook

and A, work in chain stitch over reverse Stockinette stripes on sleeves. Fasten off. Sew shoulder seams.
NECKBAND: With smaller size circular needle and MC, pick up and knit 102 (106, 110) sts around neck. Work 1-1/4" in 1/1 ribbing, bind off.
Sew sleeves to side seams, matching center of sleeve to shoulder seam. Sew side and sleeve seams.

CHART 6

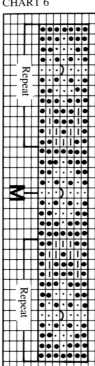

⚙⚙ ELEGANT

Ivy leaves and a trellis

pattern convert a simple

navy blue sweater into

an elegant showpiece.

SIZES

■ Small (Medium, Large)
■ Finished bust measurements: 43" (45-1/2", 47")
■ Finished length: 27"
■ Finished sleeve length: 17-3/4"

MATERIALS

■ Mayflower Cotton Light 12 (13, 13) balls Blue
■ DMC floss: 13 skeins ecru, 1 skein brown-434, 9 skeins beige-437.
■ U.S. size 3 and 5 knitting needles. 16" Circular needle U.S. size 3. (Metric sizes: 3.0, 3.75, and 3.0 40 cm. circular.)

GAUGE

U.S. size 5 needles in St st: 4" (10 cm.) = 22 sts x 29 rows.
To save time, take time to check gauge!

BACK

With smaller size needles and Blue, cast on 104 (110, 116) sts and work 2" in 1/1 ribbing. Purl 1 row on wrong side of work, inc 18 sts evenly spaced across row = 122 (128, 134) sts. Change to larger size needles, work in St st. Shape.Armholes: When back measures 16-1/2" (16", 15-3/4") from beg - 107 (104, 102) rows above border, bind off 3 sts at beg of next 2 rows. Bind off 2 sts at beg of next 2 rows. Dec 1 at each edge of every 2nd row once = 110 (116, 122) sts. Shape Shoulders: When back measures 9-3/4" (10-1/4", 10-1/2") from beg of armhole -180 rows above border, bind off 12 (12, 13) sts at beg of next 4 (4, 6) rows. Bind off 11 (13, 0)

sts at beg of next 2 rows. Bind off rem 40 (42, 44) sts for neck.

FRONT

Beg front same as back. Shape armholes as on back.
Shape Neck: When front measures 8-1/2" (9", 9-1/4") from beg of armhole -171 rows above border, bind off center 22 (24, 26) sts. Join 2nd ball of yarn to 2nd part and work at the same time. At each neck edge of every 2nd row, bind off 3 sts once, bind off 2 sts twice, dec 1 st twice.

Shape Shoulders: When front measures 9-3/4" (10-1/4", 10-1/2") from beg of armhole -180 rows above border, shape shoulders as on back.

SLEEVE

With smaller size needles and Blue, cast on 46 (48, 50) sts, work 2" in 1/1 ribbing. Purl 1 row on wrong side of work, inc 8 sts evenly spaced across row = 54 (56, 58) sts.
Change to larger size needles, work in St st. Inc 1 st each edge of every 2nd row 0 (2, 4) times. Inc 1 st each edge of every 4th row 27 (26, 25) times. Work new sts in St st as you inc = 108 (112, 116) sts.
When sleeve measures 17-3/4" from beg, end wrong side of work row.
Shape Sleeve Top: Bind off 3 sts at beg of next 6 rows. Bind off 4 sts at beg of next 2 rows. Bind off 5 sts at beg of next 4 rows. Bind off 6 sts at beg of next 4 rows. Bind off 9 (10, 11) sts at beg of next 2 rows. Bind off rem 20 (22, 24) sts.

FINISHING

Embroider the front in

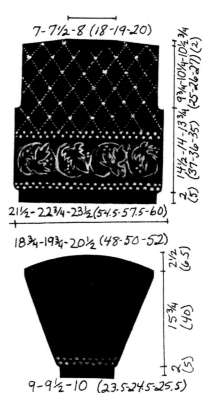

7-7½-8 (18-19-20)

14½-14-13¾ 9¾-10¼-10½ ¾ (37-36-35) (25-26-27) (2)

2 (5)

21½-22¾-23½ (54.5-57.5-60)

18¾-19¾-20½ (48-50-52)

2½ (6.5)

15¾ (40)

2 (5)

9-9½-10 (23.5-24.5-25.5)

duplicate stitch by foll chart 1, beg with 1 border st, work between point 1 to point 2, 20 (21, 22) times, end with 1 border st. Beg chart 2 on the 3rd row above chart 1: 1 border st, work from point 1 (2, 3) to point 5 once, work from point 4 to point 5 once, and from point 4 to point 6 (7, 8) once, 1 border st. Beg 4 rows from the last row of chart 2, work chart 3: work

1 border st, then point 1 (2, 3) to point 4, work from point 4 to point 5, 7 times total, end with 1 border st. Beg with the 4th row above the last row of chart 2. Work chart 3 to last row of front. Embroider the dots in stem stitch on chart 2 in ecru. Embroider the sleeves by working 2 rows of dots of chart 1. Center the chart and beg on the 3rd row above ribbing.

Embroider stems on chart 2 in stem stitch and balls in chain stitch in ecru. Sew shoulder seams. With circular needle and Blue, pick up and knit 96 (100, 102) sts around neck. Work 1-1/4" in 1/1 ribbing, bind off. Set in sleeves, matching center of sleeve to shoulder seam. Sew side and sleeve seams.

Chart 3

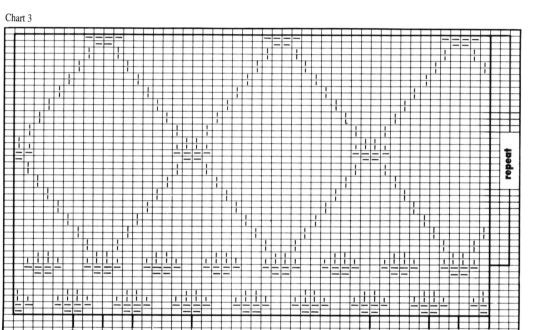

KEY TO CHARTS
☐ Blue
Ⓘ Ecru
⊟ Beige
⊙ Brown

Chart 1

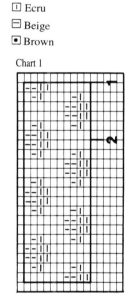

Chart 2

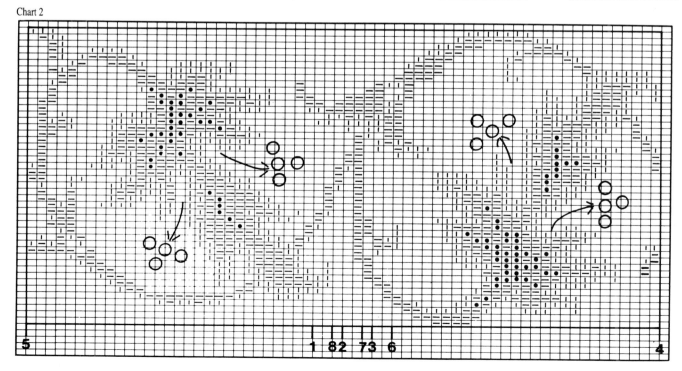

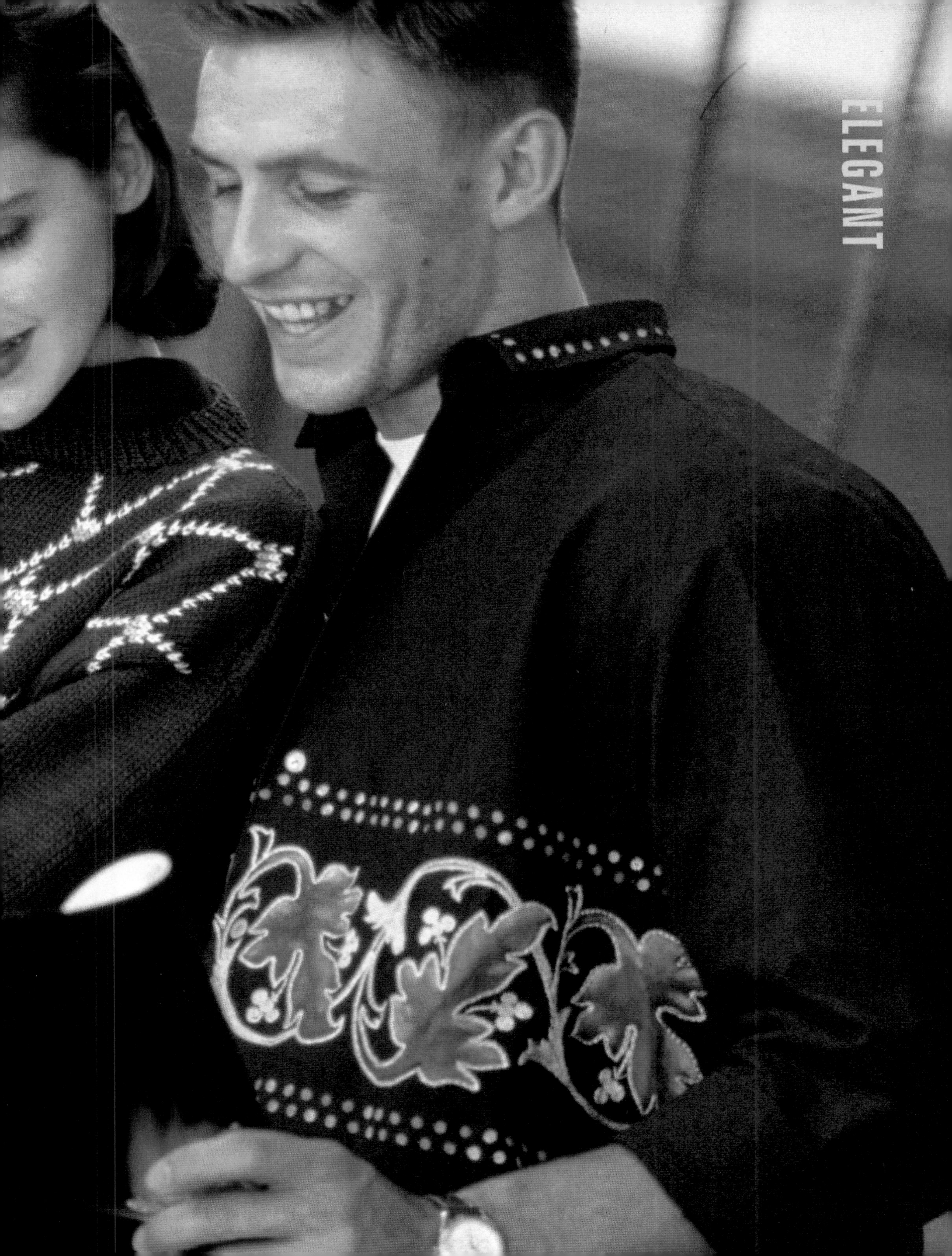

ELEGANT

✿✿ GLOWING

Bright sunflower motifs are

reminiscent of a Mexican

vacation's sunset.

SIZES
■ Small (Medium, Large)
■ Finished bust measurements: 42-1/2" (45", 47")
■ Finished length: 25-1/2"
■ Finished sleeve length: 17-3/4"

MATERIALS
■ Scheepjeswol Domino or Mayflower Felina (50 g): 11 (12, 13) balls Melon - MC; 2 balls Bright Yellow - A; 1 ball each White - B, Yellow - C, Old Gold - D, Pink - E, Green - F, Purple - G
■ U.S. size 3 and 5 knitting needles. 16" Circular needle U.S. size 3. (Metric sizes: 3.0, 3.75, and 3.0 40 cm. circular.)

GAUGE
U.S. size 5 needles in St st: 4" (10 cm.) = 22 sts x 30 rows.
To save, time take to check gauge!

BACK
With smaller size needles and MC, cast on 104 (108, 114) sts and work 2-1/2" in 1/1 ribbing, inc 17 (19, 20) sts evenly spaced across last wrong side of work row = 121 (127, 134) sts. Change to larger size needles, work in St st. (The flowers are embroidered later in duplicate stitch.)

Shape Armholes: When back measures 15" (14-1/2", 14") - 96 (93, 90) rows above border, bind off 3 sts at beg of next 2 rows. Bind off 2 sts at beg of next 2 rows. Dec 1 st at each edge of every 2nd row once = 109 (115, 122) sts.
Shape Neck: When back measures 9-3/4" (10", 10-1/2") from beg of armhole - 171 rows above border, bind off center 53 (55, 56) sts. Join 2nd ball of yarn to 2nd part and work at the same time. At each neck edge of every 2nd row, bind off 3 sts once, bind off 2 sts once. **At the same time,** Shape Shoulders: At each armhole edge of every 2nd row, bind off 9 (9, 10) sts once, bind off 7 (8, 9) sts twice.

FRONT
Beg front same as back. Shape armholes as on back. Shape Neck: When front measures 8-1/4" (8-1/2", 9") from beg of armhole - 159 rows above border, bind off center 39 (41, 42) sts. Join 2nd ball of yarn to 2nd part and work at the same time. At each neck edge of every 2nd row, bind off 3 sts once, bind off 2 sts twice, dec 1 st 5 times. Shape Shoulders: When front measures 9-3/4" (10",

10-1/2") from beg of armhole -171 rows above border, shape shoulders as on back.

SLEEVE
With smaller size needles and MC, cast on 50 (52, 54) sts, work 2" in 1/1 ribbing. Inc 10 sts evenly spaced across last wrong side of work row = 60 (62, 64) sts.
Change to larger size needles, work in St st. Inc 1 st each edge of every 4th row 18 (21, 24) times. Inc 1 st each edge of every 6th row 6 (4, 2) times. Work new sts in St st as you inc = 108 (112, 116) sts.
When sleeve measures 17-3/4" from beg, end wrong side of work row.
Shape Sleeve Top: Bind off 4 sts at beg of next 4 rows. Bind off 7 sts at beg of next 6 rows. Bind off 8 (8, 9) sts at beg of next 4 (2, 4) rows. Bind off 9 sts at beg of next 0 (2, 0) rows. Bind off rem 18 (20, 22) sts.

FINISHING
Embroider body in duplicate st by foll chart: beg with 1 border st, work point 1 (2, 3) to point 4 (5, 6), end with 1 border st. Embroider sleeves by centering chart. Sew shoulder seams. With circular needle and MC, pick up and knit 160 (166, 170) sts around neck. Work in 1/1 ribbing as foll: 1/3" in MC, 1/3" in C, 1/3" in MC, 1/3" in E, 1/3" in MC. Knit all sts on the first round of a new color. Bind off loosely. Set in sleeves, matching center of sleeve to shoulder seam. Sew side and sleeve seams.

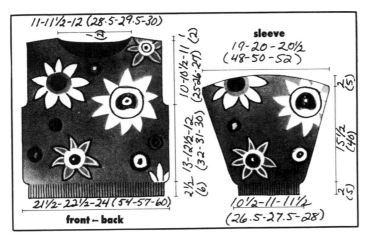

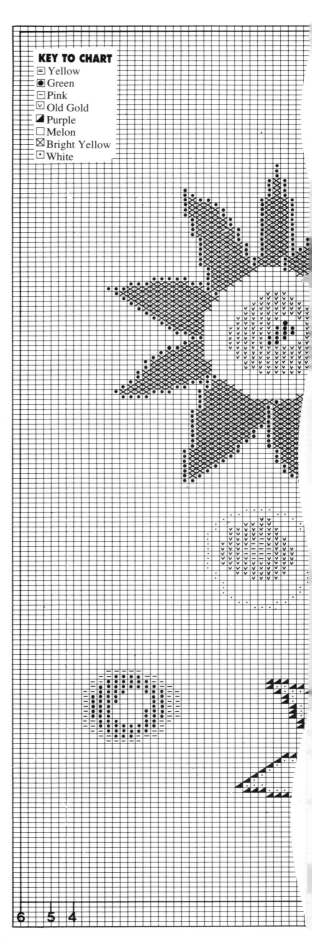

KEY TO CHART
⊟ Yellow
⦿ Green
⊟ Pink
⊡ Old Gold
◪ Purple
☐ Melon
⊠ Bright Yellow
⊡ White

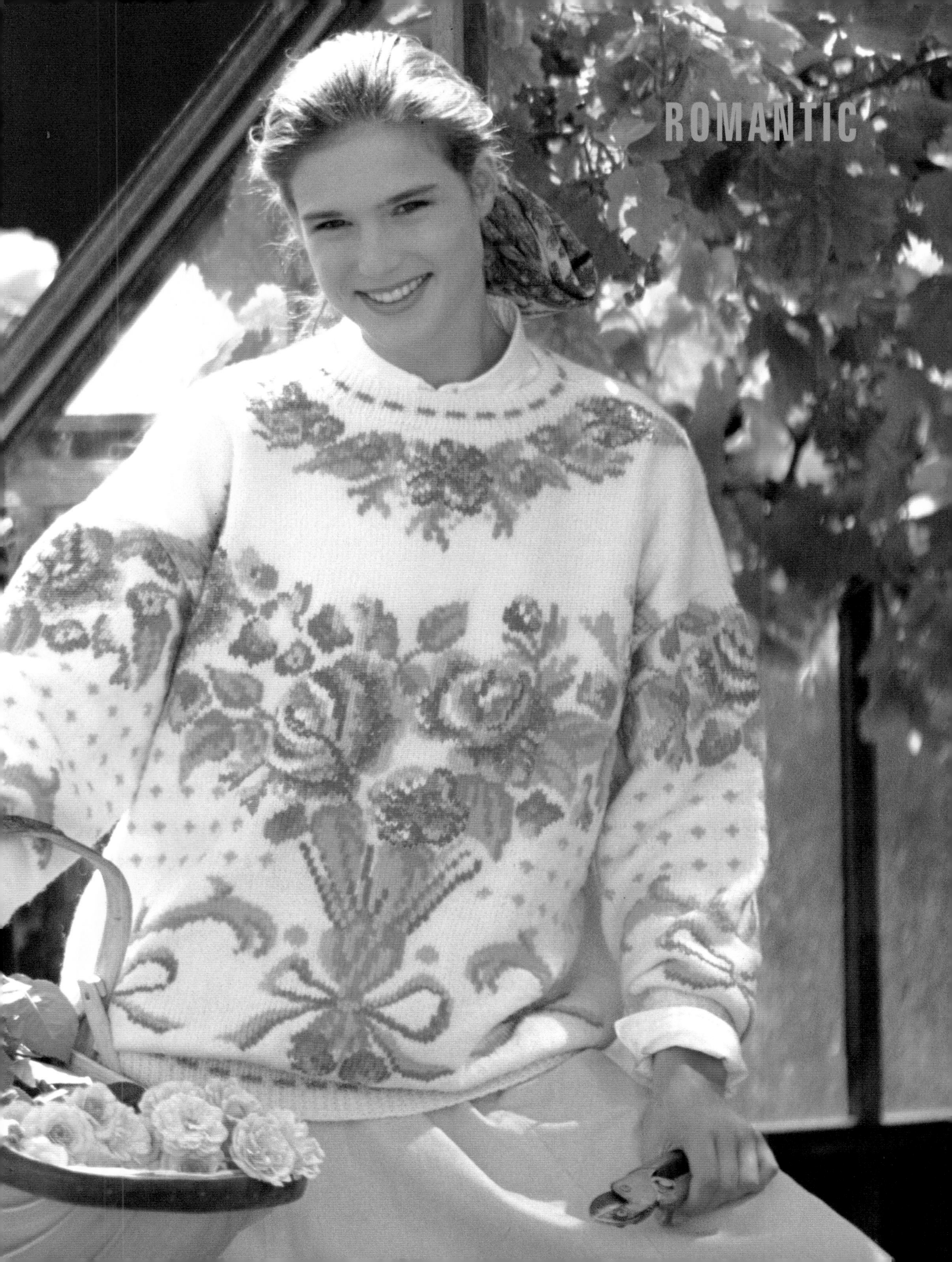
ROMANTIC

⚙ ROMANTIC

Beautiful bouquets of roses and ribbons were embroidered in duplicate stitch over a fairisle background.

SIZES
- Small(Medium, Large)
- Finished bust measurements: 45" (48", 51")
- Finished length: 27-1/2"
- Finished sleeve length: 17-3/4"

MATERIALS
- Stahl Limbo Superwash (50 g): 11 (12, 13) balls Ecru - MC; 1 ball each Dark Rose - A, Light Rose - B, Red - C, Lilac - D, Purple - E, Light Blue - F, Medium Blue - G and Dark Blue - H
- Anchor Tapestry wool: 17 skeins light green-569, 5 skeins green-579
- U.S. size 2 and 4 knitting needles. 16" Circular needle U.S. size 2. (Metric sizes: 2.5, 3.5, and 2.5 40 cm. circular.)

GAUGE
U.S. size 4 needles in St st: 4" (10 cm.) = 23 sts x 33 rows.
To save time, take time to check gauge!

BACK
With smaller size needles and MC, cast on 116 (122, 128) sts and work in 1/1 ribbing as foll: work 1" in MC, then work next row as foll: 1 border st, 2 sts in F, *2 sts in MC, 4 sts in F*, rep * to *, end with 2 sts in MC, 2 sts in F, 1 border st. Work foll row in established colors. Continue in MC in 1/1 ribbing until piece measures 2-1/2". Purl 1 row across wrong side of work, inc 17 (20, 23) sts evenly spaced across row = 133 (142, 151) sts.
Change to larger size needles, work in St st as foll: 9 rows following chart 1, beg with 1 border st, point 1 (2, 3) to point 4 (5, 6), end with 1 border st. Work vertically from point A to point B, complete in MC. Knit in the green leaves above ribbing and the green crosses. Carry unused yarn loosely across wrong side of work. Embroider flowers and bow motifs later in duplicate stitch.
Shape Armholes: When back measures 17" (16-1/2", 16") from beg - 122 (119, 116) rows above border, at each edge of every 2nd row, dec 1 st once, bind off 2 sts once, dec 1 st once = 125 (134, 143) sts.
Shape Neck: When back measures 9-3/4"(10-1/4", 10-1/2") from beg of armhole-205 rows above ribbing, point G on chart, bind off center 33 (36, 39) sts. Join 2nd ball of yarn to 2nd part and work at the same time. At each neck edge of every 2nd row, bind off 3 sts twice. **At the same time,**
Shape Shoulders: At armhole edge of every 2nd row, bind off 13 (14, 15) sts twice, bind off 14 (15, 16) sts once.

FRONT
Beg front same as back. Work chart as foll: 1 border st, then work by foll chart 1, beg with 1 border st, then point 1 (2, 3) to point 4 (5, 6), end with 1 border st. Beg at row marked A. Complete in MC. When piece measures 17" (16-1/2", 16") from beg - point C (D, E) on chart, shape armholes as on back = 125 (134, 143) sts.

Shape Neck: When armhole measures 8-1/4" (8-1/2", 9") from beg - point F on chart, bind off center 19 (22, 25) sts. Join 2nd ball of yarn to 2nd part and work at the same time. At each neck edge of every 2nd row, bind off 3 sts once, bind off 2 sts 3 times, dec 1 st 4 times. When armhole measures 9-3/4" (10-1/4", 10-1/2") from beg - point G on chart, at each armhole edge of every 2nd row, bind off 13 (14, 15) sts twice, bind off 14 (15, 16) sts once.

SLEEVE
With smaller size needles and MC, cast on 50 (50, 56) sts, work 2-1/2" in 1/1 ribbing as on back. Purl 1 row on wrong side of work, inc 12 (13, 10) sts evenly spaced across row = 62 (63, 66) sts.
Change to larger size needles, work in St st, centering charts at M (M1, M). Work green leaves and green crosses only foll chart 2. After 4 repeats of green crosses, foll chart 1 for placement of crosses,

omitting crosses where flower motif will be embroidered later. **At the same time,** inc 1 st each edge of every 4th row 16 (22, 25) times. Inc 1 st at each edge of every 6th row 9 (5, 3) times. Work new sts in St st as you inc = 112 (117, 122) sts.
When sleeve measures 17-3/4" from beg, end wrong side of work row.
Shape Sleeve Top: Bind off 3 sts at beg of next 2 rows. Bind off 4 sts at beg of next 10 rows. Bind off 5 (5, 6) sts at beg of next 2 rows. Bind off 6 (7, 7) sts at beg of next 4 rows. Bind off rem 32 (33, 36) sts.

FINISHING
Embroider flowers in duplicate st on front by foll chart 1. Embroider sleeves as foll: embroider 1 blue bow beg 20 rows above ribbing. (Center one of the smaller side bows of chart 1.) Embroider green motif foll chart 3 on the first row above the bow, centering at point M (M1, M). Embroider the flower motif by foll chart 2. Sew shoulder seams. Neckband: With circular needle and MC, pick up and knit 114 (114, 120) sts around neck. Work 1/2" in 1/1 ribbing in MC, then work 2 rounds in 1/1 ribbing as foll: *2 sts in MC, 4 sts in F*, rep * to * around. Continue in MC until neckband measures 1-1/4". Bind off.
Set in sleeves, matching center of sleeve to shoulder seam. Sew side and sleeve seams.

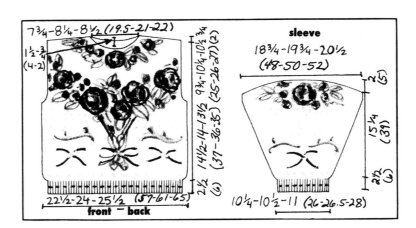

KEY TO CHART
- ☐ MC
- ☒ A
- ⊙ B
- ◡ C
- ◿ D
- ☐ E
- ▽ F
- ☒ G
- ≈ H

repeat   MM1   repeat

CHART 1 - upper left

NOTE: Chart 1 is in four sections. Xerox all four sections and tape together.

KEY TO CHART

☐ MC
☑ A
⊡ B
⌴ C
◺ D
⌊ E
▽ F
☒ G
⊠ H

CHART 1 - upper right

G

F

C
D
E

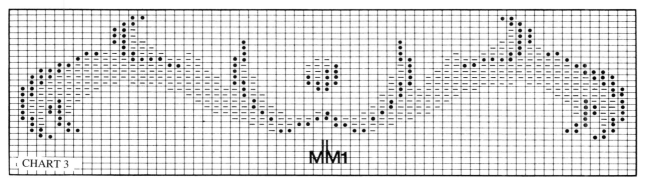

CHART 3

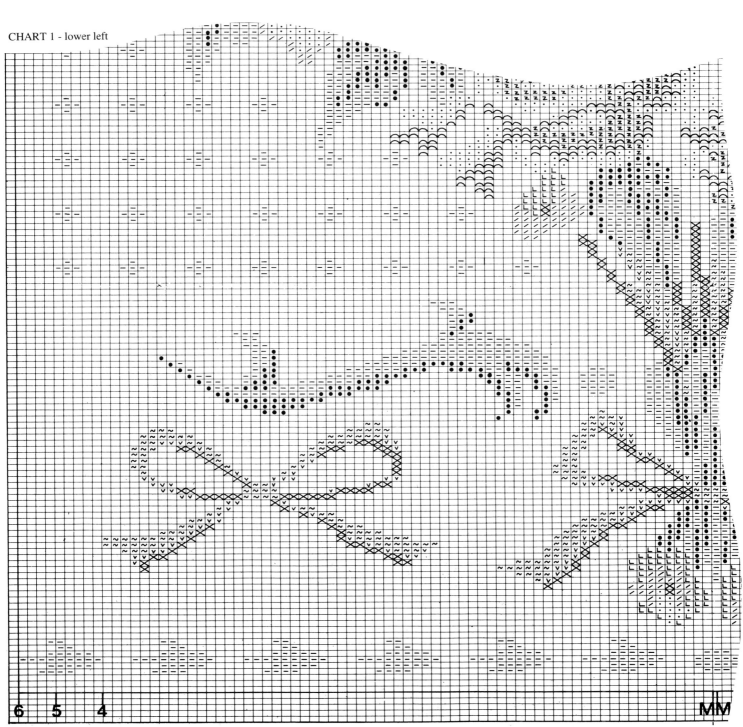

CHART 1 - lower left

6 5 4

KEY TO CHARTS

☐ MC
☑ A
☑ B
☐ C
☑ D
☐ E
☑ F
☒ G
☑ H

CHART 1 - lower right

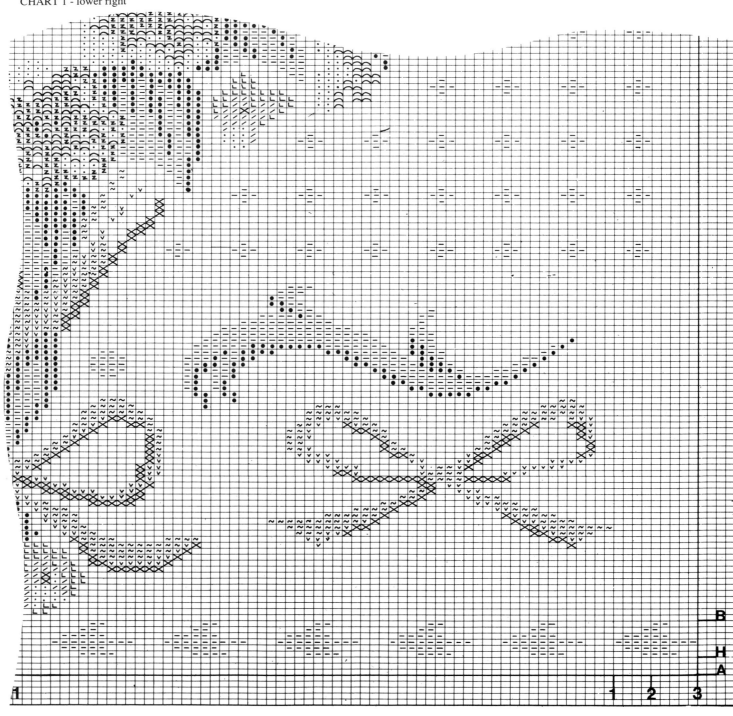

COUNTRY

Pretty flowers are sprinkled

over stripes in this lucky

little girl's sweater..

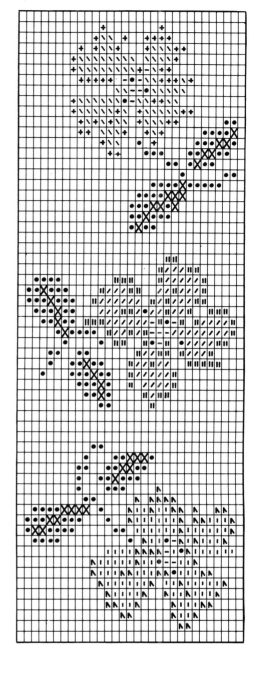

SIZES
- 2 (4, 6, 7) years
- Finished chest measurements: 24-1/2" (26-1/2", 28", 30")
- Finished length: 14-3/4" (16", 18", 19-3/4")
- Finished sleeve length: 9-1/2" (10-3/4", 12", 13-1/4")

MATERIALS
- Mayflower Cotton 8 (50 g): 3 (3, 4, 4) balls White - MC; 2 balls Turquoise - A; 1 (2, 2, 2) balls Lilac - B
- DMC Embroidery Floss: Dark Salmon - 353, Dark Rose - 603, Rose - 605, Green - 702, Light Green - 704, Yellow - 726, Salmon Rose - 754, Blue - 799 and Light Blue - 800.
- U.S. size 2 and 3 knitting needles. (Metric sizes: 2.5 and 3.0.) 4 buttons.

GAUGE
U.S. size 3 needles in St st: 4" (10 cm.) = 26 sts x 36 rows.
To save time, take time to check gauge!

BACK
With smaller size needles and B, cast on 72 (76, 80, 84) sts and work 1-1/2" in 1/1 ribbing. Purl 1 row on wrong side of work, inc 11 (14, 16, 17) sts evenly spaced across row = 83 (90, 96, 101) sts.
Change to larger size needles and work in striped St st as foll: 4 (4, 8, 4) rows in MC, *2 rows A, **2 rows MC, 2 rows A**, work ** to ** 3 times, 8 rows MC*, work * to * throughout.
When back measures 13-1/2" (15", 17", 18-1/2")

from beg, change to smaller size needles and B and work 1 row in St st, then work in 1/1 ribbing.
Shape Neck: When back measures 1-1/4" from beg of ribbing, bind off center 37 (40, 42, 43) sts. Join 2nd ball of yarn to 2nd part and work at the same time. When ribbing measures 2-1/2", bind off rem 23 (25, 27, 29) sts on each shoulder.

FRONT
Beg front same as back. When top ribbing measures 1/2", make buttonholes as foll: right side facing, work 9 (10, 11, 12) sts, bind off 2 sts, work 8 (9, 10, 11) sts, bind off 2 sts, work to last 21 (23, 25, 27) sts, bind off 2 sts, work 8 (9, 10, 11) sts, bind off 2 sts, work to end of row. On foll row, cast on 2 sts over bound off sts. Work until ribbing measures 1-1/4", bind off loosely.

SLEEVE
With smaller size needles and B, cast on 38 (40, 42, 44) sts, work 1-1/2" in 1/1 ribbing. Purl 1 row on wrong side of work, inc 15 (15, 17, 19) sts evenly spaced across row = 53 (55, 59, 63) sts.
Change to larger size needles and work in striped St st as on back. At the same time, inc 1 st each edge of every 4th (4th, 4th, 8th) row 9 (6, 4, 1) time. Inc 1 st each edge of every 6th row 5 (9, 12, 15) times. Work new sts in striped St st as you inc = 81 (85, 91, 95) sts.
When sleeve measures 9-

1/2" (10-3/4", 12", 13-1/4") from beg, bind off all sts.

FINISHING
Embroider flower motifs as you desire on front, back and sleeves in duplicate stitch. Overlap shoulder seams and tack in place at armhole edge. Sew sleeves to side seams, matching center of sleeve to center of shoulder. Sew side and sleeve seams. Reinforce buttonholes and sew on buttons.

KEY TO EMBROIDERY CHART
- ⊙ Light Green - 704
- ⊠ Green - 702
- ⊟ Salmon - 754
- ◹ Dark Salmon - 353
- ☑ Rose - 605
- ⊞ Dark Rose - 603
- ◲ Light Blue - 800
- ⊟ Blue - 799
- ⊡ Yellow - 726

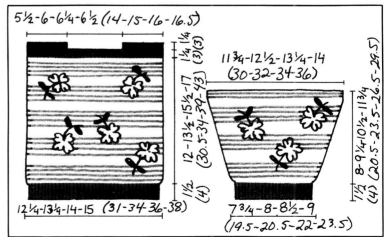

COMPLEMENT

COMPLEMENT

A richly-embroidered

cardigan complements

the subtle embroidery on

the pullover and skirt.

KEY TO CHART, SKIRT

- ☒ = Pink
- ⊙ = Fuchsia
- ◪ = Light Green
- ◣ = Dark Green

SKIRT

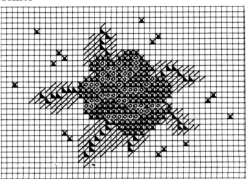

CARDIGAN

MATERIALS

■ Purchased pink cardigan about 19-3/4" long, exclusive of lower ribbing and neckband.
■ 2 pieces of 20 count linen 6-1/2" x 19-3/4".
■ Embroidery floss: 1 skein each light green, dark green, light blue, dark blue.

Pin the linen pieces against outside over the left front edge of cardigan, allowing 1-1/4" from button border. Beg at lower edge at point A and work each cross stitch over 2 threads. Work through the linen and the knitted sweater. Reverse the chart to correspond on the right front. Cut away unused linen.

PULLOVER

MATERIALS

■ Purchased yellow pullover with neck width about 17" around.
■ 1 piece of 20 count linen 20" x 2-1/2".
■ Embroidery floss: 1 skein each light green, dark green, light blue.

Pin the linen pieces against the outside of front and back neck edge of pullover. Beg at lower edge of chart at point M about 2-1/2" from top of center front neck edge and work each cross stitch over 2 threads. Work through the linen and the knitted sweater. Work same motif on back neck. Cut away unused linen.

SKIRT

MATERIALS

■ Purchased blue knit skirt. 1 piece of 20 count

linen 3-1/2" x 4-3/4" for each motif.
■ Embroidery floss: 1 skein each pink, fuchsia, light green, dark green.

Pin the linen pieces against outside of skirt 3" from lower edge. Embroider the

motif, working each cross stitch over 2 threads. Work through the linen and the knitted skirt. Work as many motifs as desired. Cut away unused linen.

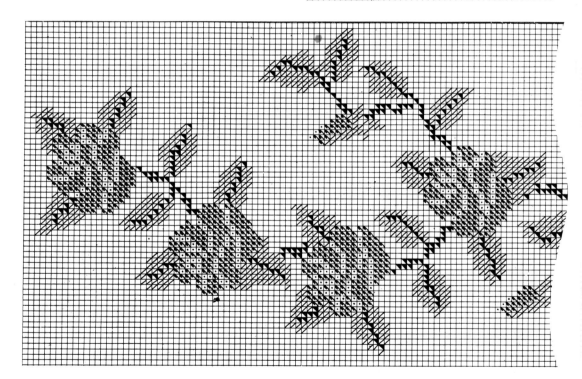

KEY TO CHART, PULLOVER
◨ = Light Green
⊡ = Light Blue
◤ = Dark Green

KEY TO CHART, CARDIGAN
◹ = Light Green
◪ = Dark Green
⊡ = Light Blue
◨ = Dark Blue

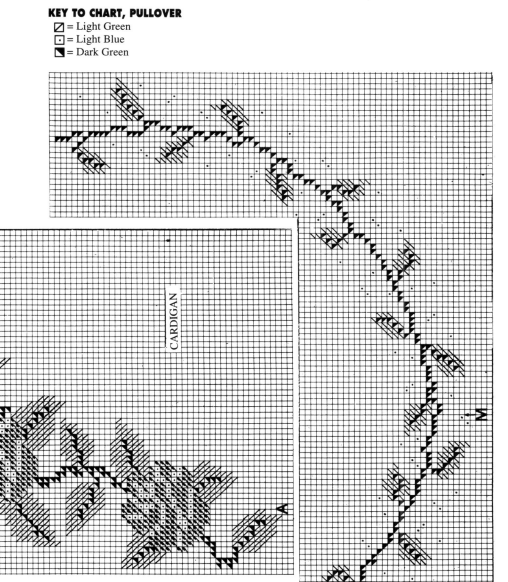

CARDIGAN

PULLOVER

SATIN

A classic dress-up cardigan

for a little girl was created

with duplicate stitch

embroidery.

SIZES
- 6 (8, 10) years
- Finished chest measurements: 29" (30-1/2", 33")
- Finished length: 17-1/4" (18-3/4", 20-3/4")
- Finished sleeve length: 9-3/4" (10-3/4", 12")

MATERIALS
- Scheepjeswol Soft Elegance (50 g): 5 (6, 7) balls Ecru - MC; 2 balls each Pink - CC
- DMC embroidery floss: dark brown-301, red-349, dark salmon-352, salmon-353, light brown-402, light blue-519, dark green-562, green-563, dark blue-825, blue-826, light blue-828, brown-922, light green-955, rose-3705, ecru. 2-1/2 yards white ribbon 1/3" wide.
- U.S. size 3 and 5 knitting needles. (Metric sizes: 3.0 and 3.75.)

GAUGE
U.S. size 5 needles in St st: 4" (10 cm.) = 23 sts x 33 rows.
To save time, take time to check gauge!

BACK
With smaller size needles and CC, cast on 88 (92, 98) sts and work 3/4" in St st. Right side facing, work 1 row in eyelet stitch as foll: 1 border st, *k2 tog, yo*, rep * to *, end with 1 border st. Purl foll row, including yos.
Change to larger size needles, work in St st. work 16 (18, 20) rows in CC, then complete in MC.
Shape Armholes: When back measures 11" (12-1/4", 13-3/4") from beg, bind off 2 sts at beg of next 2 rows. Dec 1 st at each edge of every 2nd row twice = 80 (84, 90) sts.
Shape Neck: When armhole measures 6-1/2" (7", 7-1/2") from beg, bind off center 30 (32, 34) sts. Join 2nd ball of yarn to 2nd part and work at the same time. At each neck edge of every 2nd row, bind off 2 sts once. When back measures 18" (19-3/4", 21-1/2") from beg, bind off rem 23 (24, 26) sts on each shoulder.

RIGHT FRONT
With smaller size needles and CC, cast on 40 (42, 46) sts and work border as on back.
Change to larger size needles in St st as foll: 16 (18, 20) rows in CC, complete in MC.
Shape Armhole: When front measures 11" (12-1/4", 13-3/4") from beg, at armhole edge of every 2nd row, bind off 2 sts once, dec 1 st twice = 36 (38, 42) sts.
Shape Neck: When front measures 5-1/2" (6", 6") from beg of armhole, at neck edge of every 2nd row, bind off 0 (4, 4) sts once, bind off 3 sts 3 (2, 2) times, bind off 2 sts once, dec 1 st 2 (2, 4) times. When front measures 18" (19-3/4", 21-1/2") from beg, bind off rem 23 (24, 26) sts on shoulder.

LEFT FRONT
Work same as right front, rev shapings.

SLEEVE
With smaller size needles and CC, cast on 50 (52, 54) sts, work border as on back.
Change to larger size needles, work in St st as foll: 13 (15, 17) rows in CC,

complete in MC. At the same time, work even until piece measures 1-1/2", then inc 1 st each edge of every 4th row 10 (12, 11) times. Inc 1 st each edge of every 6th row 5 (5, 7) times = 80 (86, 90) sts. Work new sts in St st as you inc.
When sleeve measures 11-1/4" (12-1/2", 13-1/2") from beg, end wrong side of work row.
Shape Sleeve Top: Bind off 4 sts at beg of next 2 rows. Bind off 5 (6, 6) sts at beg of next 4 rows. Bind off 7 sts at beg of next 2 rows. Bind off 9 (9, 10) sts at beg of next 2 rows. Bind off rem 20 (22, 24) sts.

FINISHING
Embroider the flower border in duplicate stitch by foll chart 1 at lower edge of fronts and back. Back: work 1 border st, then work from point 1 (2, 3) to point 4 (5, 6), 1 border st. For the right front, work 1 border st, point 7 (1, 8) to point 9, 1 border st. For the left front, work 1 border st, point 10 to point 11 (4, 12), 1 border st. Beg embroidery on the 9th (11th, 13th) row above the eyelet row. Embroider the sleeves by centering chart 1. Beg embroidery on the 8th (10th, 12th) row above eyelet row. Embroider flowers over the back, fronts and sleeves wherever you desire by foll chart 2, using the photo as a guide. Sew shoulder seams. Set in sleeves, matching center of sleeve to shoulder seam. Sew side and sleeve seams. Fold borders at eyelet row to inside and slip stitch in place. With smaller size needles, pick up and knit 88 (96, 100) sts along right front edge, matching colors and work in St st. When border measures 3/4" from

beg, end wrong side of work row. Work 1 row of eyelets, then work until border measures 1-1/2" total, bind off. Work same border on left front edge. Fold borders to inside and slip stitch in place. With smaller size needles and MC, pick up and knit 80 (84, 88) sts around neck and work same border as on lower edge. Bind off. Fold in half to inside and slip stitch in place. Cut 10 (10, 12) pieces of ribbon 8" long. Sew ribbons to front, evenly spaced, using photo as a guide.

KEY TO CHARTS
- ⬚ and 9 = pink
- ▣ and 8 = ecru
- Embroidery floss:
- ⊘ ecru
- ⊡ light brown
- ⊠ brown
- ⊞ dark brown
- ⊟ light green
- • green
- ◪ dark green
- ⊡ bright blue
- ⊟ light blue
- ⊠ blue
- ■ dark blue
- ⊡ salmon
- ◹ dark salmon
- ◹ rose
- ⊠ red

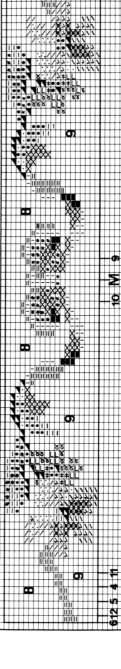

Chart 1

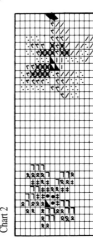

Chart 2

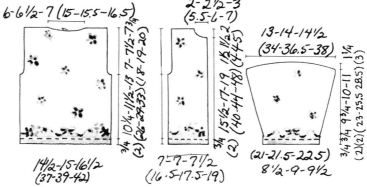

124

❧ PLAYFUL

This soft baby pullover with knitted-in horizontal stripes and crocheted vertical stripes is accented with a floral motif.

SIZES
- 3 (6, 12) months
- Finished chest measurements: 22" (23", 23-1/2")
- Finished length: 11" (11-1/2", 11-3/4")
- Finished sleeve length: 6-1/2" (7-1/4", 8")

MATERIALS
- Scheepjeswol Voluma (50 g): 2 balls Beige - MC; 1 ball each Tan - A and Lilac - B
- Tapestry wool: 1 skein each: pink, dark pink, yellow, green, dark green, light sea green, sea green, salmon, orange, dark orange.
- U.S. size 4 and 6 knitting needles. Circular needle U.S. size 6, 24" long. Crochet hook U.S. size C/2. (Metric sizes: 3.5, 4.0, and 4.0 60 cm. circular; crochet hook 3.0.) 2 buttons.

GAUGE
U.S. size 6 needles in St st: 4" (10 cm.) = 22 sts x 31 rows.
To save time, take time to check gauge!

FRONT
With smaller size needles and A, cast on 64 (66, 68) sts and work in 1/1 ribbing as foll: 1 row A, *2 rows B, 2 rows A*, work * to * twice total.
Change to larger size circular needle and work back and forth in St st as foll: *8 rows MC, 1 row A*, rep * to *. Beg at edge where the correct color yarn hangs.
Shape Neck: When front measures 9 1/4" (9-3/4", 10-1/4") from beg, bind off center 22 (24, 26) sts. Join

2nd ball of yarn to 2nd part and work at the same time. At each neck edge of every 2nd row, bind off 2 sts once, dec 1 st twice.
Shape Shoulders: When front measures 10" (10-1/2", 10-3/4") from beg of armhole, bind off rem 17 sts on each shoulder.

BACK
Beg back same as front.
Shape Neck: When back measures 10-1/2" (11", 11-1/2") from beg, bind off center 30 (32, 34) sts. Join 2nd ball of yarn to 2nd part and work at the same time. At each neck edge of every 2nd row, bind off 3 sts once, bind off 2 sts 7 times. At the same time, 3 rows from the first neck shaping, make a buttonhole. Beg at neck edge, work 1 border st, work 3 sts, k2 tog, yo, work to end of row. When back measures 10" (10-1/2", 10-3/4") from beg of armhole, bind off all sts.

SLEEVE
With smaller size needles and A, cast on 28 (30, 32) sts, work in 1/1 ribbing, inc 8 sts evenly spaced across last wrong side of work row = 36 (38, 40) sts.

Change to larger size needles, work in striped St st as foll: 6 (7, 7) rows in A; 2 rows in B; 4 (5, 5) rows in MC; 2 (2, 3) rows in A; 3 rows in MC; 7 (8, 9) rows in B; 2 rows in MC; 1 row alternately 1 st in orange tapestry wool and 1 st in MC; 1 row in MC; 2 (3, 4) rows in B; 3 rows in A; 1 row alternately 1 st in A, 1 st in light green tapestry wool; 4 (5, 6) rows in MC; 8 (8, 9) rows in A = 46 (51, 56) rows. **At the same time**, inc 1 st each edge of every 6th row 1 (4, 6) times. Inc 1 st each edge of every 4th row 9 (6, 4) times. Work new sts in St st as you inc = 56 (58, 60) sts.
When sleeve measures 6-3/4" (7-1/4", 7-3/4") from beg, bind off all sts.

NECKBAND
With smaller size needles and A, pick up and knit 65 (67, 69) sts along front neck and work 1/2" in 1/1 ribbing. Bind off loosely.
With smaller size needles and A, pick up and knit 79 (81, 83) sts along back neck and work 1/2" in 1/1

ribbing. Bind off loosely.

FINISHING
Embroider flower motif in duplicate stitch on front, working the first st 20 (21, 22) sts from right edge and 12 (14, 16) rows from above border. Crochet the vertical bands as foll: beg at left edge, work 1 stripe between the 7th and 8th (8th and 9th, 9th and 10th) sts in light sea green. Work the foll 6 (6, 7) stripes 8 sts apart as foll: pink, green, orange, light sea green, pink, green and orange. Crochet as foll: with yarn at back of work, pull a loop to front side with crochet hook. Insert hook from front to back 2 rows above first loop and pull through yarn, then pull this loop through the first loop. Continue in this way, skipping flower motif sts and continuing to neck. Fasten off. Overlap the back shoulder borders over front and tack shoulder edges in place. Sew sleeves to side seams, matching center of sleeve to center of shoulder. Sew side and sleeve seams. Sew on buttons.

KEY TO CHART
- ⊡ Rose
- ⊟ Dark Rose
- ⊙ Yellow
- ◪ Green
- ◩ Dark Green
- ⊠ Light Green
- ◨ Sea Green
- ⊡ Salmon
- ◨ Orange
- ⬛ Dark Orange

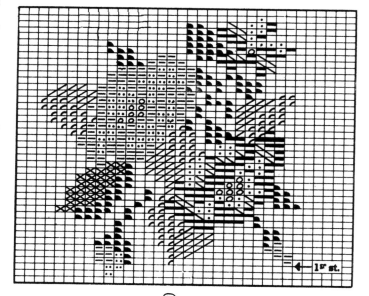

5½-6-6¼
(14-15-16)

8½-9-9½
(22-23-24)

¾
(2)

11-11½-11¾
(28-29-30)

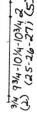

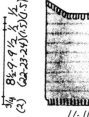

9¾-10¼-10¾
(25-26-27)

½
(1.5)

¾
(2)

11-11½-11¾
(28-29-30)

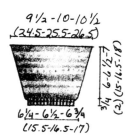

9½-10-10½
(24.5-25.5-26.5)

6-6½-7
(15-16.5-18)

¾
(2)

6¼-6½-6¾
(15.5-16.5-17)

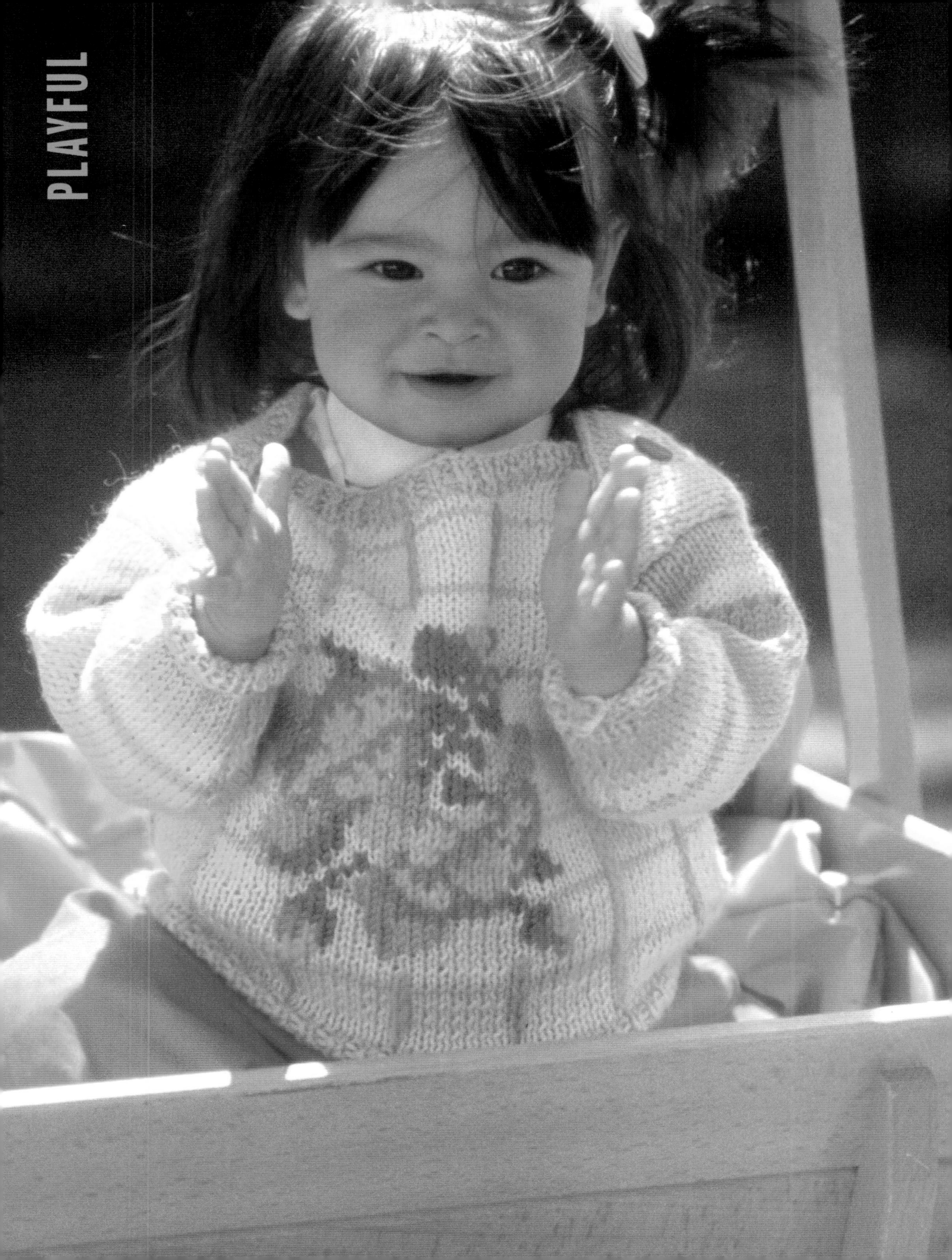

TREASURE

This ecru sweater jacket is decorated with knitted bobbles and large embroidered flowers and foliage.

SIZES
- Small (Medium, Large, X-Large)
- Finished bust measurements: 43" (45-1/2", 47-1/2", 50")
- Finished length: 28"
- Finished sleeve length: 17" (17-1/4", 17-3/4", 18")

MATERIALS
- Scheepjeswol Superwash Zermatt (50 g): 17 (18, 18, 19) balls Ecru
- Anchor tapestry wool: 5 skeins lilac-095, green-0242, 4 skeins pink-0642, 3 skeins lilac-085, tuquoise-0567, dark green-0257, 2 skeins gold-3013
- U.S. size 3 and 5 knitting needles. (Metric sizes: 3.0 and 3.75.)

GAUGE
U.S. size 5 needles in St st: 4" (10 cm.) = 21 sts x 28 rows.
To save time, time time to check gauge!

BACK
With smaller size needles and Ecru, cast on 117 (123, 129, 135) sts and work 1-1/2" in St st, then work 1 row as foll: *k1, p1*, rep * to * across. Change to larger size needles and continue in St st until piece measures 3-1/4" from beg. End on wrong side of work row. Work foll row as foll: 1 border st, k5 (4, 4, 3), *1 bobble (all in 1 st: k1, p1, k1, p1, k1, turn, sl 1, p4, turn, sl 1, k4, turn, sl 1, p4, turn, k5 tog), k6*, work * to * 15 (16, 17, 18) times total, 1 bobble, k4 (4, 3, 3), 1 border st. Continue in St st.
Shape Armholes: When back measures 19-1/4"

(18-3/4", 18-1/2", 18") from beg - 115 (112, 109, 106) rows above bobble row, bind off 3 sts at beg of next 2 rows. Bind off 2 sts at beg of next 2 rows. Dec 1 st at each edge of every 2nd row once = 105 (111, 117, 123) sts.
Shape Neck: When back measures 9-1/4" (9-3/4", 10-1/4", 10-1/2") from beg of armhole-182 rows above bobble row, bind off center 27 (29, 31, 33) sts. Join 2nd ball of yarn to 2nd part and work at the same time. At neck edge of every 2nd row, bind off 7 sts once, bind off 2 sts once. **At the same time,** Shape Shoulders: At each armhole edge of every 2nd row, bind off 12 (12, 12, 14) sts once, bind off 9 (10, 11, 11) sts twice.

FRONT
Beg front same as back.
Shape Neck: When front measures 7-3/4" (8", 8-1/2", 8-3/4") from beg of armhole - 169 rows above bobble row, bind off center 13 (15, 17, 19) sts. Join 2nd ball of yarn to 2nd part and work at the same time. At each neck edge of every 2nd row, bind off 4 sts twice, bind off 3 sts once, bind off 2 sts twice, dec 1 st once.
Shape Shoulders: When front measures 9-1/4" (9-3/4", 10-1/4", 10-1/2") from beg of armhole, shape shoulders as on back.

SLEEVE
With smaller size needles and Ecru, cast on 38 (38, 42, 42) sts, work 1-1/4" in 2/2 ribbing as foll, wrong

side facing: 1 border st, p1, *k2, p2*, rep * to * across, end with k2, p1, 1 border st. Purl 1 row on wrong side of work, inc 15 (17, 15, 17) sts evenly spaced across row = 53 (55, 57, 59) sts.
Change to larger size needles, work in St st. On the 9th row above ribbing, work bobble row as foll: 1 border st, k3 (4, 1, 2), *1 bobble, k6*, rep * to * 6 (6, 7, 7) times, 1 bobble, k2 (3, 1, 2), 1 border st, continue in St st. **At the same time,** inc 1 st each edge of every 4th row 17 (18, 20, 22) times. Inc 1 st each edge of every 6th row 6 (6, 5, 4) times. Work new sts in St st as you inc = 99 (103, 107, 111) sts. When sleeve measures 17" (17-1/4", 17-3/4", 18") from beg-112 (115, 118, 120) rows above bobble row, end wrong side of work row.
Shape Sleeve Top: Bind off 4 sts at beg of next 2

rows. Bind off 3 sts at beg of next 4 rows. Bind off 4 sts at beg of next 4 rows. Bind off 5 sts at beg of next 2 rows. Bind off 6 sts at beg of next 2 rows. Bind off 7 sts at beg of next 2 rows. Bind off rem 27 (31, 35, 39) sts.

FINISHING
Embroider motifs on body by foll chart 1 and on sleeves foll chart 2. Begin the embroidery on the body 4 rows above the bobble row and on the 4th (6th, 8th, 10th) row above bobble row on the sleeves. Center chart 1, omitting the outside circles for the 2 smallest sizes. Center chart 2. Embroider the lines in stem stitch, the circles in satin stitch and the crosses in cross st using photo as a guide for placement and colors. Embroider in turquoise 1 row above ribbing on the sleeves, each V covering 4 sts and 4 rows and spaced 2 sts apart. Em-

broider in turquoise 1 row above ribbed row on the lower edge of body, each V covering 2 sts and 3 rows, spaced 2 sts apart. Sew right shoulder seam. With larger needle and MC, pick up and knit 100 (106, 114, 119) sts around neck and work in St st as foll: 1 row in MC, 1 row in lilac, 1 row as foll: 1 border st, *7 (6, 7, 6) sts in lilac, 7 sts in ecru*, rep * to * , 1 border st. Work foll 2 rows in established colors, then work 2 rows in lilac, 1 row in ecru. On the last row, dec 2 (0, 0 ,1) st. Change to smaller size needle and Ecru and work in 2/2 ribbing for 6". Bind off loosely. Sew left shoulder and neckband seam. Fold neckband in half to inside and slip stitch in place. Set in sleeves. Sew side and sleeve seams. Fold lower edge to inside at ribbed row and sew in place.

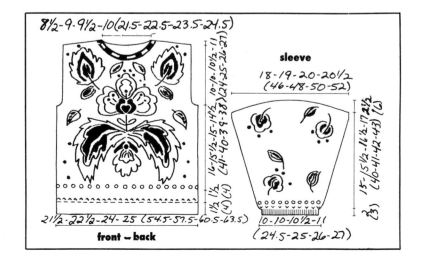

8½-9-9½-10 (21.5-22.5-23.5-24.5)

10-15½-15-14½ (40-40.3-38)

10-10-10½-11 (24.5-26-27)

21½-22½-24-25 (54.5-57.5-60.5-63.5)

front ~ back

sleeve
18-19-20-20½ (46-48-50-52)

15-15½-16½-17-17½ (40-41-42-43) (3)

10-10-10½-11 (24.5-25-26-27)

Chart 1

NOTE:
Embroider the lines in stem stitch, the circles in satin stitch, the crosses in cross stitch, using photo as a guide for placement and color.

NOTE:
Embroider the lines in stem
stitch, the circles in satin stitch,
the crosses in cross stitch, using
photo as a guide for placement
and color.

Chart 2

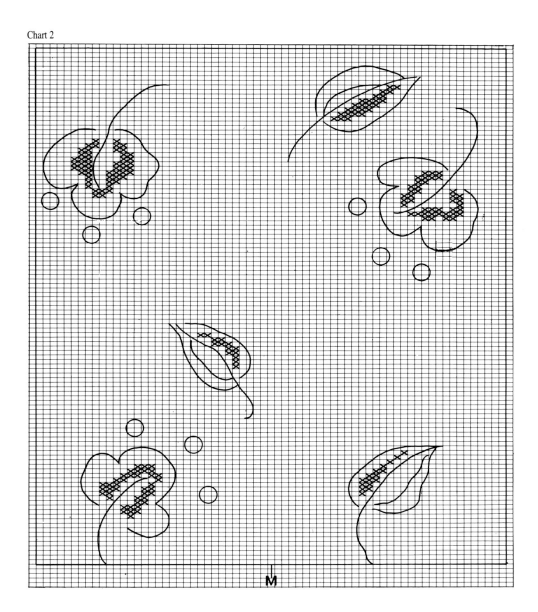

⚙ SUNNY

Wildflowers are scattered

between zigzag borders on

this child's pullover.

SIZES
■ 6 (7, 8) years
■ Finished chest measurements: 29" (30", 31")
■ Finished length: 18" (18-3/4", 20")
■ Finished sleeve length: 12-1/2" (13-1/4", 13-3/4")

MATERIALS
■ Mayflower Cotton 8 (50 g): 5 (6 ,6) balls White - MC; 1 ball each Green - A, Light Rose - B, Rose - C and Bright Green - D
■ DMC Embroidery Floss: yellow - 973, orange - 970, purple - 553, lilac - 554, light green - 955, blue gray - 519 and turquoise - 996.
■ U.S. size 2 and 3 knitting needles. (Metric sizes: 2.5 and 3.0.) 4 buttons.

GAUGE
U.S. size 3 needles in St st: 4" (10 cm.) = 26 sts x 36 rows.
To save time, take time to check gauge!

BACK
With smaller size needles and MC, cast on 97 (101, 105) sts and work 1-1/4" in St st, then work 1 row of eyelets on right side of work as foll: 1 border st, *k2 tog, yo*, rep * to * across, end with k1, 1 border st. Purl 1 row, purling all yos. Work 10 rows foll chart 1, beg with 1 border st, work from point 2 (1, 3) to point 5 once and from point 4 to point 5, 7 (7, 8) times and point 4 to point 7 (8, 6) once, 1 border st. Carry unused color across wrong side of work. When chart is complete work 1 row of eyelets. Change to larger size nee-

dles and MC and work in St st until back measures 16-3/4" (17-1/2", 18-3/4") above eyelet row. Work 10 rows of chart 1. Back will measure 18" (18-3/4", 20") above eyelet row.
Change to smaller size needles and B and work 1-1/4" in 1/1 ribbing: 1/3" in B, 1/3" in MC, 1/3" in B. Bind off loosely.

FRONT
Beg front same as back. When front measures 18" (18-3/4", 20") above eyelet row, change to smaller size needles and B. Work 1 row in St st, then work in 1/1 ribbing as on back. Always work the first row of a new color in St st. At the same time, when border measures 1/2", make 4 buttonholes as foll: right side facing, work 10 (11, 11) sts, bind off 3 sts, work 10 (10, 11) sts, bind off 3 sts, work 45 (47, 49) sts, bind off 3 sts, work 10 (10, 11) sts, bind off 3 sts, work 10 (11, 11) sts. On the foll row, cast on 3 sts over bound off sts. Bind off loosely.

SLEEVE
With smaller size needles and B, cast on 42 (44, 46) sts and work 1/3" in B, *1/3" in MC, 1/3" in B*, work * to * twice total, end with wrong side of work row. Work first row of new color in St st.
Purl 1 row in B across wrong side of work, inc 18 (18, 17) sts evenly spaced across row = 60 (62, 63) sts. Change to larger size needles and work as foll: 2 rows in MC, 10 rows foll chart 1, centering at point

M (M, M1). Complete in MC. At the same time, inc 1 st each edge of every 4th row 9 (6, 7) times. Inc 1 st each edge of every 6th row 9 (12, 12) times. Work new sts in St st as you inc = 96 (98, 101) sts.
When sleeve measures 12-1/2" (13-1/4", 13-3/4")

from beg, bind off all sts.

FINISHING
Embroider the front and back in duplicate st by centering chart 2 and beg chart on the 5th (8th, 13th) row above eyelet row. Center chart 3 on sleeves at point M (M, M1), beg on the 5th

(8th, 10th) row above the last row in ribbing. Overlap front ribbing over back and tack ends in place. Sew sleeves to side seams, matching center of sleeve to center of shoulder. Sew side and sleeve seams. Reinforce buttonholes and sew on buttons.

Chart 1

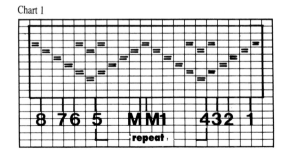

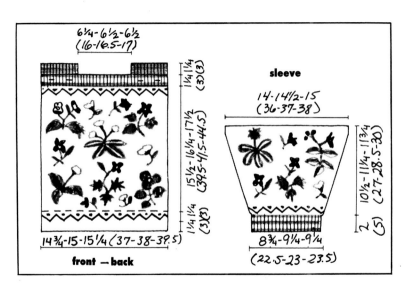

6¼-6½-6½
(16-16.5-17)

14 1¼
(3)(3)

15½-16¼-17½
(39.5-41.5-44.5)

1¼ 1¼
(3)(3)

14¾-15-15¼ (37-38-39.5)

front — back

sleeve

14-14½-15
(36-37-38)

10½-11¼-11¾
(27-28.5-30)

2
(5)

8¾-9¼-9¼
(22.5-23-23.5)

KEY TO EMBROIDERY CHARTS

☐ White
◩ Purple
⊠ Turquoise
⊟ Blue
⬠ Orange
⬚ Yellow
⬛ Light Green
⬤ Green
⬜ Bright Green

Chart 3

134

KEY TO EMBROIDERY CHARTS

- ☐ White
- ◪ Purple
- ⊠ Turquoise
- ⊟ Blue
- ⬃ Orange
- ⊑ Yellow
- ⊡ Light Green
- ⊙ Green
- ⧄ Bright Green

Chart 2

CHARM

A flattering neckline adds to the old-fashioned charm of this floral sweater.

SIZES
- Small (Medium, Large)
- Finished bust measurements: 41" (44", 47")
- Finished length: 26"
- Finished sleeve length: 17-1/2"

MATERIALS
- Mayflower Cotton 8 (50 g): 9 (10, 11) balls Light Peach
- DMC embroidery floss: 11 skeins white, 5 skeins purple-340, 7 skeins light purple-341, 12 skeins green-368, 8 skeins light green-369, 7 skeins gold-676, 12 skeins light gold-677, 5 skeins dark rose-760, 13 skeins old rose-761, 12 skeins light rose-963.
- U.S. size 1 and 2 knitting needles. 16" Circular needle U.S. size 1 and 2. (Metric sizes: 2.0, 2.5, and 2.0 and 2.5 40 cm. circular.)

GAUGE
U.S. size 2 needles in St st: 4" (10 cm.) = 27 sts x 35 rows.
To save time, take time to check gauge!

BACK
With smaller size needles and Light Peach, cast on 122 (130, 138) sts and work 1-1/2" in 1/1 ribbing. Purl 1 row across wrong side of work, inc 20 (23, 26) sts evenly spaced row = 142 (153, 164) sts. Change to larger size needles, work in St st. Shape Raglans: When back measures 16" (15-1/2", 15-1/4") from beg - 127 (124, 121) rows above ribbing, bind off 3 sts at beg of next 2 rows. *Dec 1 st at each edge of every first, 2nd,

4th, 5th, 7th row*, work * to * 7 times total. At each edge of every row, dec 1 st 2 (5, 8) times as foll: Right side facing: 1 border st, sl 1, p1, psso, work to last 3 sts, k2 tog, 1 border st. Wrong side facing: 1 border st, sl 1, k1, psso, work to last 3 sts, sl 1 st onto cable needle and hold at front of work, sl the foll st onto the right hand needle, slip the first st from the cable needle onto the left hand needle and with the right hand needle, p2 tog, 1 border st.
Shape Neck: When back measures 4-1/4" (4-3/4", 5") from beg of raglan - 166 rows above ribbing, bind off center 42 (47, 52) sts. Join 2nd ball of yarn to 2nd part and work at the same time. At each neck edge of every 2nd row, bind off 3 sts twice, bind off 2 sts once, dec 1 st twice. After the last raglan decrease, piece will measures 21-1/2" - 178 rows above ribbing.

FRONT
Beg front same as back. Work raglans as on back. Shape Neck: When front measures 3-3/4"(4-1/4", 4-1/2") from beg of raglan - 161 rows above ribbing, bind off center 26 (31, 36) sts. Join 2nd ball of yarn to 2nd part and work at the same time. At each neck edge of every 2nd row, bind off 4 sts 3 times, bind off 2 sts twice, dec 1 st twice.

SLEEVE
With smaller size needles and Light Peach, cast on 56 (58, 60) sts, work 1-1/2" in 1/1 ribbing. Purl 1

row on wrong side of work row, inc 21 sts evenly spaced across row = 77 (79, 81) sts.
Change to larger size needles, work in St st. Inc 1 st each edge of every 4th row 16 (22, 28) times. Inc 1 st each edge of every 6th row 11 (7, 3) times. Work new sts in St st as you inc = 131 (137, 143) sts.
When sleeve measures 17-1/2" from beg - 142 rows above ribbing, end wrong side of work row.
Shape Raglans: Bind off 3 sts at beg of next 2 rows. Dec 1 st at each edge of every row 0 (0, 3) times. *Dec 1 st at each edge of every first and 3rd row*, work * to * 15 (18, 18) times. Dec 1 st at each edge of every 2nd row 3 (0, 0) times.
At the same time, when raglan measures 4-3/4" (5", 5-1/4") - 43 (46, 49) rows from beg of raglan, bind off center 33 sts. Join 2nd ball of yarn to 2nd part

and work at the same time. At each edge of every 2nd row, bind off 6 sts once, bind off 4 sts once, bind off 3 sts once.

FINISHING
Embroider flowers by centering chart on front and back at point M (M1, M). Center the chart at point X on sleeves. Use 4 strands of embroidery floss to embroider in duplicate stitch. Where 2 colors are used, use 2 strands of each color. Sew raglan seams. Neckband: With larger size circular needle and Light Peach, pick up and knit 206 (216, 226) sts around neck. Work 2" in 1/1 ribbing, change to smaller size circular needle and continue in 1/1 ribbing until neckband measures 4-1/4". Change to larger size circular needle and work until neckband measures 6-1/4" total, bind off. Fold neckband to outside. See photo. Sew side and sleeve seams.

KEY TO CHART
- □ white
- ◪ 760
- ⊟ 761
- ◻ 963
- ⊞ 761 + 963
- ⊠ 340
- ⊞ 341
- ◻ 677
- ◙ 676
- ⊠ 761 + 677
- ◿ 677 + 676
- ⊟ 677 + 963
- ⊠ 368
- ◻ 369
- ▣ 368 + 369

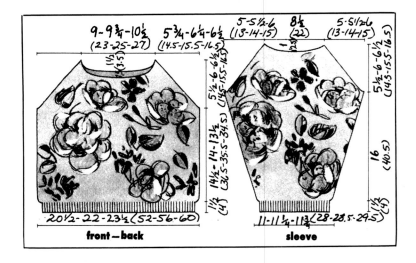

9-9¾-10½ (23-25-27) 5¾-6¼-6½ (14.5-15.5-16.5) 5-5½-6 (13-14-15) 8½ (22) 5-5½-6 (13-14-15)

(1½) (3.5)

14½-14-13¾ (36.5-35.5-34.5) 5½-6-6½ (14.5-15.5-16.5) 5½-6-6½ (14.5-15.5-16.5)

1½ (4) 16 (40.5) 1½ (4)

20½-22-23½ (52-56-60) 11-11¼-11¾ (28-28.5-29.5)

front—back   **sleeve**

KEY TO CHART

- ⊡ white
- ◪ 760
- ⊟ 761
- ◺ 963
- ⊞ 761 + 963
- ⊠ 340
- Ⅲ 341
- ⊡ 677
- ⊡ 676
- ⊠ 761 + 677
- ⊘ 677 + 676
- ⊡ 677 + 963
- ⊠ 368
- ⊡ 369
- ❋ 368 + 369

M

A Spring bouquet of wildflowers adorns the pocket and the back of this embroidered cardigan knit in a Stockinette stitch — perfect for hand or machine knitting.

SIZES

- Small (Medium, Large)
- Finished bust measurements: 41-1/2" (45", 48")
- Finished length: 24-1/2" (25-1/2", 26-1/4")
- Finished sleeve length: 17-3/4"

MATERIALS

- Neveda Skol (50 g): 11 (13, 14) balls White - MC 1 ball Blue - CC
- DMC Embroidery Floss: green - 320, salmon - 353, light green - 472, yellow - 726, dark lavender - 792, lavender - 793, rose - 3326 and old rose - 3328
- U.S. size 2 and 4 knitting needles. Circular needle U.S. size 2. (Metric sizes: 2.5, 3.5, and 2.5 circular.) 6 buttons.

GAUGE

U.S. size 4 needles in St st: 4" (10 cm.) = 23 sts x 31 rows.
To save time, take time to check gauge!

BACK

With smaller size needles and MC, cast on 112 (120, 128) sts and work 1-1/4" in St st, end wrong side row. Knit 2 rows in CC. Change to MC and work until piece measures 2-1/2" from beg. Purl 1 row on wrong side of work, inc 12 (13, 14) sts evenly spaced across row = 124 (133, 142) sts.
Change to larger size needles, work in St st. Shape Armholes: When back measures 14-3/4" (15-1/4", 15-1/2") from beg - 98 (101, 104) rows from inc row, bind off 3 sts at beg of next 2 rows, bind off 2 sts at beg of next 2 rows. Dec 1 st at each edge of every 2nd row once = 112 (121, 130) sts.
Shape Neck: When back measures 10-1/4" (10-1/2", 11") from beg of armhole - 178 (185, 191) rows from inc row, bind off center 28 (31, 34) sts. Join 2nd ball of yarn to 2nd part and work at the same time. At each neck edge of every 2nd row, bind off 4 sts once, bind off 3 sts once.
At the same time,
Shape Shoulders: At each armhole edge of every 2nd row, bind off 11 (12, 13) sts once, bind off 12 (13, 14) sts twice.

RIGHT FRONT

With smaller size needles and MC, cast on 54 (58, 62) sts and work border as on back. Purl 1 row on wrong side of work, inc 6 (6, 7) sts evenly spaced across row = 60 (64, 69) sts.
Change to larger size needles and work in St st. Shape Armhole: When front measures 14-3/4" (15-1/4", 15-1/2") from beg, at armhole edge of every 2nd row, bind off 3 sts once, bind off 2 sts once, dec 1 st once. Work dec as foll: k1, sl 1, k1, PSSO, work to end of row.
At the same time,
Shape Neck: When front measures 15-1/2" (16", 16-1/4") from beg, at neck edge of every 2nd row, dec 1 st 0 (0, 2) times. At neck edge of every 4th row, dec 1 st 19 (20, 20) times. **At the same time,**
Shape Shoulder: When front measures 10-1/4" (10-1/2", 11") from beg of armhole, at armhole edge of every 2nd row, bind off 11 (12, 13) sts once, bind off 12 (13, 14) sts twice.

LEFT FRONT

Work same as right front, rev shapings. Work dec as foll: work to last 3 sts, K2 tog, K1.

SLEEVE

With smaller size needles and MC, cast on 56 (58, 60) sts, work border as on back. Purl 1 row on wrong side of work, inc 7 (8, 8) sts evenly spaced across row = 63 (66, 68) sts. Change to larger size needles, work in St st. Inc 1 st each edge of every 4th row 20 (23, 26) times. Inc 1 st each edge of every 6th row 7 (5, 3) times. Work new sts in St st as you inc = 117 (122, 126) sts.
Shape Sleeve Top: When sleeve measures 19" from beg, bind off 3 sts at beg of next 2 rows. Bind off 4 sts at beg of next 4 rows. Bind off 5 sts at beg of next 4 rows. Bind off 6 sts at beg of next 4 rows. Bind off 7 (8, 8) sts at beg of next 2 (4, 2) rows. Bind off 8 (0, 9) sts at beg of next 2 rows. Bind off rem 21 (24, 26) sts.

POCKET

With larger size needles and MC, cast on 27 sts and work 4-1/2" - 35 rows in St st, end wrong side of work row. Knit 2 rows in CC. Change to smaller size needles and continue in MC until piece measures 5-3/4" from beg, bind off loosely.

FINISHING

Embroider back and pocket in duplicate st centering charts. Center chart 1 on back at point M (M1, M) and beg embroidery on the 4th (7th, 10th) row above the inc row at lower edge. Embroider the line using a single strand of Dark Lavender in outline stitch. Embroider the flowers on the pocket by centering chart 2, beg embroidery on the 2nd row. Sew shoulder seams. With circular needle and MC, pick up and knit 148 (156, 164) sts around left front edge + 1 st at center back neck. Work 1-1/4" in 1/1 ribbing, end wrong side of work row. Change to CC and knit 2 rows. Change to MC and continue until ribbing measures 2-1/2" total. Bind off. On the right front, make the same border, making 6 buttonholes when piece measures 1/2" and 2". Make the first buttonhole 1/2" from lower edge and top buttonhole at the beg of V-Neck with 4 buttonholes evenly spaced between them. For each buttonhole, bind off 3 sts. On foll row, cast on 3 sts above bound off sts. Sew back neck seam. Set in sleeves. Sew side and sleeve seams. Fold all borders to inside and slip stitch in place. Sew pocket to center of left front, 12-1/4" (12-1/2", 13") above folded edge. Sew on buttons.

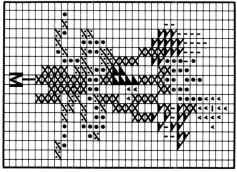

Chart 2

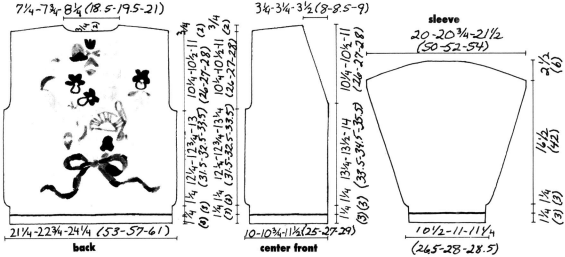

7¼-7¾-8¼ (18.5-19.5-21)

3¼-3¼-3½ (8-8.5-9)

sleeve 20-20¾-21½ (50-52-54)

3¾ (9)

10¼-10½-11 (26-27-28)

10¼-10½-11 (26-27-28)

10¼-10½-11 (26-27-28)

7¼ (8)

7¼ (8)

12¼-12¾-13 (31.5-32.5-33.5)

12¼-12¾-13¼ (31.5-32.5-33.5)

13¼-13½-14 (33.5-34.5-35.5)

2½ (6)

16½ (42)

1¼ (3)

1¼ (3)

back

center front

21¼-22¾-24¼ (53-57-61)

10-10¾-11½ (25-27-29)

10½-11-11¼ (26.5-28-28.5)

141

Chart 1

MM1

142

BIBLIOGRAPHY

Bredewold, Ank, and Pleiter, Anneke. *The Knitting Design Book.* Asheville, North Carolina: Lark Books, 1988.

Hiatt, June Hemmons. *The Principles of Knitting.* New York City, New York: Simon and Schuster, 1988.

Goldberg, Rhoda Ochser. *The New Knitting Dictionary.* New York City, New York: Crown Publishers, 1984.

Theiss, Nola. *Glorious Crocheted Sweaters.* New York City, New York: Sterling Publishing Co., 1989.

The Reader's Digest Complete Guide to Needlework. Pleasantville, New York: The Reader's Digest Association, 1979.

BUYER'S GUIDE

Mayflower Cottons, Scheepjeswol and Neveda Yarns:
Mayflower Yarn USA/
Holland Spinneries
P.O. Box 1046
Clarksville, MD 21029
301-854-3537
800-447-3537

Jaeger Wild Silk:
Jaeger Handknitting Yarns
212 Middlesex Avenue
Chester, CT 06412

Rowan Yarn:
Westminster Trading Corp.
5 Northern Boulevard
Amherst, NH 03031

Stahl Yarn:
Skacel Collection
224 SW 12th St.
Renton, WA 98055

INDEX